THE PSALMS

THE PSALMS

*A New Translation
for Prayer
and Worship*

Translated by

GARY CHAMBERLAIN

THE UPPER ROOM
Nashville, Tennessee

THE PSALMS: A New Translation for Prayer and Worship

Book design: Harriette Bateman
First printing: September 1984 (5)
Library of Congress Catalog Card Number: 84-50842
ISBN 0-8358-0485-2
Printed in the United States of America

Contents

Preface

The primary purpose of this book is to introduce a new translation of the Book of Psalms specifically intended for private and public prayer. The text itself, then, is where the readers' attention should be directed, and I will not place in their way the obstacle of a long introduction. Still, the psalms do present difficulties, and comparison with other translations may raise questions of method and purpose in the minds of those who peruse almost any portion of this rendering. So I have included three brief essays before the psalms themselves. The first is intended to assist those who find the psalms troublesome as personal prayers. The second contains some observations on psalms for corporate worship. The third presents a few examples of how specific translation problems were addressed. Those wishing more extensive treatment of these issues will have little trouble in finding much to read about the psalms; while those who are not yet, or no longer, troubled by such things can proceed directly to the psalms themselves.

Any book is in truth the work of many people, and it is not empty traditionalism or false humility, but simple honesty, that compels authors to recognize that their own personal contribution consists largely of foibles, errors, and the willful and perverse misunderstanding of what others have tried to teach them. So it is with this book.

It is the whole scholarly community, through hundreds of books that I have consulted, that is primarily responsible for the shape of the text. This is not the type of work for which one cites bibliography or constructs masses of footnotes, but I admit that there is hardly anything here that I did not glean from someone else. On two members of the scholarly fellowship I have been more personally dependent: Dr. Stephen Szikszai, who first introduced me to Hebrew, and Dr. H. Neil Richardson, who guided my graduate study. They can stand as exemplars of all who have been, less directly, my teachers.

Nevertheless, the primary focus of this work was not scholarship but prayer, particularly prayer in the devotion and public worship of local congregations. As Karl Barth did sixty years ago, I must thank my parishioners for enduring my commitment to study and my obsessive interest in one biblical book. That I had the time or energy to do the work at all is solely the result of their financial, personal, and spiritual support. Brackett Memorial Church, on Peaks Island, has sustained the work for the last two years. Before that, Pratt Memorial Church in Rockland and Peoples Church in South Thomaston encouraged me to begin and to continue. In purely practical terms, this Psalter is the costly gift of three small congregations on the coast of Maine on behalf of their whole denomination, and this book is dedicated to them.

I also want to express my gratitude to my secretary, Deborah Vondras, not only for assisting me with her technical skills, but even more for the encouragement of her interest in the psalms themselves. The psalms have become more important to me than I can say, and the long labor of translation has been more than repaid by my sense of special relationship with the church's central book of prayer. That Debi is challenged and enriched by the results strengthens my hope that there will be others who may meet God in these prayers.

The Psalms As Prayers

There are only two biblical texts which most Christian congregations are able to recite from memory—the Lord's Prayer and Psalm 23. Both of them are prayers, even though the psalm is a meditative reflection *about* God, rather than a statement *to* God.

Perhaps we do not think of the psalms as prayers, although that is precisely what they have been through the entire history of the church. (That is why in congregational worship they are not read as "scripture lessons," but recited or sung by the whole congregation.) And that is what they have become for me. My personal prayer is more and more firmly based in the psalms. If I try to pray out of my own mind and heart, I am at a loss after a few minutes, and my mind wanders away from God. Praying the psalms keeps my attention, draws my prayer in many different directions that I would not have taken on my own, and gives me many opportunities to listen as well as speak. Prayer becomes genuine conversation, in which I say things I did not know I wanted to say to anyone (let alone God!), and hear words addressed to me which I know I did not imagine or invent.

I want to say here a few things about my experience of praying the psalms. They are often things that other people have also said; I have been especially helped by the writings of Thomas Merton and Dietrich Bonhoeffer. But I won't say anything here that I have not found to be true *for me*, so that this will not be a scholar's report on other people's experience, but more a direct and personal witness.

Prayer is terribly difficult. Although there is nothing we need or want more than prayer, it is the hardest thing for us to do, and probably the easiest thing to deceive ourselves about. True prayer is nothing other than attention to God, the God whom we cannot see or hear, the God who eludes all our imaginings and logical constructions, the God who makes us and demands our complete love. It is so easy to suppose that the rambling talks we toss in God's direction and the warm feelings we conjure up by our religious fantasies are true prayer and devoted love. But they are not. Those people who say that religious faith is nothing but human invention and comforting self-delusion are too often right! True faith means losing all our illusions about God and ourselves, and few of us are willing to do so. For all of us, it is a long and painful process, in which prayer becomes difficult and tedious, and God seems more and more remote.

That is why the psalms are so important. They are the prayers we need when we seem to have nothing to say to God. They are also the prayers we need when we have *many* things to say to God—all of them false, though we don't even know it! The disciples who lived with Jesus daily still needed to be *taught* how to pray. So do we.

From the psalms I have learned to pray. They are not the prayers I would have expected. They have taught me that I had many false ideas about prayer, some of which I am very reluctant to abandon. But the strength of the psalms is that they drive us toward reality.

When we begin to pray the psalms, the first thing we notice is that they are numerous, and some at least are very long. We did not know there was so much that we and God had to say to each other! Our first temptation is to be satisfied with a few psalms we already know—1, 23, 100, 121. But that is a mistake. We need some pattern for reading and learning them. We may find that one of the two patterns in *The Book of Common Prayer* of the Episcopal Church will help—to read the psalms morning and evening, completing the whole book in a month, or in seven weeks. I needed to read the whole of the psalms many times before I began to know and love some of the psalms that are now among my favorites. But our second temptation to error is to think that we ever will *enjoy* all the psalms. They are very troubling! Some I still don't like after reading the whole Psalter more than two hundred times. Our feelings of liking or not liking particular psalms are not important. In fact, the important thing is to learn the reality of prayer that does not depend on my moods or enjoyments. Psalm 123 is about loneliness and alienation. I do not want to be alienated or lonely. And when I am, I don't want to think about it. I never *enjoy* this psalm. Yet I know its power from sharing it with a friend who began to cry (the only time I have ever seen him cry) because it expressed so clearly the experiences he was enduring.

Or take Psalm 49—a meditation on the inevitability of death. The whole psalm is slightly sarcastic in tone. (I have expressed this by the heirs "remember them fondly" rather than the traditional "name their names above ground.") What a surprising mood and theme for prayer— the necessity of death, with ironic references to those who deny mortality!

In fact, the psalms continually surprise us (and may shock and distress us) by what they say. The daily language of business (Psalm 44: God doesn't "make a profit") and law (Psalm 72: the hills and mountains are the "jury") is not our usual way of speaking to God. We are even more surprised to find angry sarcasm actually directed toward God (Psalm 10: "Search out their guilt— or can't you find it?")! And the biggest obstacle for many people has been the hatred for enemies, and the prayers that they should be brutally punished.

Our minds recoil from such images as bathing our feet in blood (Psalm 58) or smashing children against a cliff (Psalm 137). The more we try to pray these psalms, the more it seems God must passionately oppose our saying such things, and reject our prayers completely.

But let us consider this problem with some care. We do not want this problem to become an excuse (as it is for some people I know) for rejecting the whole of the psalms—or even the whole of the Old Testament! Yet we cannot believe, having read of the suffering servant in Isaiah 49 and 53, that such deeds of vengeance were ever God's true purpose and will.

What would we be saying, then, if we refused to pray the psalms of vengeance? *Partly* we would be saying that people of faith, in the Old Testament or in the light of the cross of Christ, should not do such things as slaughter small children. But I would respond: Does the fact that we shouldn't do it keep us from *wanting* to do it? Are we never angry? Are we never willing to hurt or crush or humiliate someone who wrongs us? You may respond: Yes, but I shouldn't feel angry. God wants us not to feel anger, but to feel love.

I answer: Well then, are you never angry at someone you love? Are you sure that anger is not possible even while you love? And does the love that God demands of us have to do with emotions, or with deeds?

I have come to these conclusions. First, God commands us to love one another in the way we behave, not in the way we feel. Second, even when I feel great love for someone, I can be very angry. Third, when I feel guilty about my anger, I can make myself stop feeling angry— but I don't stop being angry, and the anger comes out in unexpected and sometimes very destructive ways.

So I pray the psalms of anger and revenge, because sometimes that is honestly what I want. "Break their jaws!" (Psalm 3); "Break their arms!" (Psalm 10). "Show them that I was right and they were wrong! How I would love to see them suffer! If only I could be there when they realize. . . ." And so on. I'm not saying God will do those things, nor that God wants me to do them. But if I am hurt and humiliated and angry, *God wants me to say so*. Prayer is not real unless it is honest. When we are dishonest our prayer is corrupted and our hurt and anger are left to go on as before. Then we make cutting remarks, or rationalize deceit and cruelty, or drive our cars as though we were caged beasts. Or we nurse our belligerence by identifying some "enemy" so evil that mutual nuclear annihilation becomes possible. (If we stay angry long enough, it will become likely.) Remarkably, we who are too "religious" to pray angry prayers have become the largest producer of weapons in the world.

I am not saying if we all just prayed more there would be no conflict in the world. I am saying that conflict is far more deadly when we lack the courage to know our own motives and fears, and name them to the God who can change them.

One last point. You may be a person whom everyone likes, who lives free of enmity and hostility within or without. (I have never met such a person, but for the sake of this discussion, I grant the possibility.) You may therefore never pray the psalms of hostility and revenge (or even of alienation and abandonment) as your *personal* prayers. And indeed few of us have enough anger to go to some of the extremes in which the psalms indulge (Psalms 58 and 109 are good examples). So it is crucial to remember that the psalms were prayers of the community, and not just of individuals. Jews in exile in strange lands certainly knew all the repression, cruelty, harassment, and danger that the psalms speak of. Persecuted Christians in the early church certainly felt more fearfully and cruelly assaulted by the world than we do, and were often correspondingly passionate in desiring that their enemies be punished. And today, Christians and Jews in many nations—Poland and the Soviet Union, South Korea and the Philippines, El Salvador and Lebanon and Iran—face pressures we can scarcely imagine. Not only the psalms of vengeance or abandonment, but also the psalms that pray for justice in government (Psalm 72), for wisdom and patience in trying times (Psalms 77 and 89), psalms that recall God's past deeds as signs of hope for things to come (Psalms 105–107)—all of these are our prayers shared with suffering fellow believers in our time.

This dimension of prayer for others has become real to me through a wonderful combination of circumstances. While translating the psalms, I was also doing some Bible study with a prisoners' group at the Maine State Prison. I have translated the beginning of Psalm 42: "Blessed are those who *know they are helpless.*" Most other translations say, "who *remember* the helpless" or "the poor." My translation is confirmed by the rest of the psalm, that speaks not of someone acting justly (as does Psalm 112), but of someone in profound distress. I have never felt the way the psalmist feels in Psalm 41. Yet it is an important prayer for me because of the way it spoke to some alcoholics in that prison group. Their whole experience is in it—the physical illness and deterioration, the betrayed relationships, the paranoid fear of other people and their purposes. And the promise of healing is also there; my first line corresponds to the first of the twelve steps of Alcoholics Anonymous, admitting that you have lost control of your life. The prisoners called Psalm 41 "the AA Psalm," and that is what it is for me every time I read it. It may never be my prayer, but it is our prayer, and I pray it on behalf of my brothers in Christ who wait in prison for their freedom and their Lord.

The Psalms As Songs

The psalms belong to us, not as praying individuals but as members of the assembly of God in Judaism and the Christian church. These community prayers have more often been sung than said, and a recovery of psalm prayer in our time probably depends on the broad use of sung psalms in our congregations. The psalms were sung in ancient Judaism, as we know from the frequent references to singing (Psalm 96) and musical instruments (Psalm 150). They were sung for most of Christian history by monks who chanted all the psalms every week. We need to find ways to sing them today, if only because words set to music go so much deeper into us than words that are only spoken.

We are already doing more psalm singing than most of us realize. Anthems and hymns are more often based on texts from Psalms than from any other book of the Bible. For instance, the United Methodist *Book of Hymns* index shows more references to Psalms than to all four Gospels combined! The psalms' range of theme, from praise and thanksgiving to calm reflection to grief and despair, is a constant invitation to poets and musicians, and of course the composing and singing of psalm-based songs should continue.

But we need also to sing the psalms themselves, just as all church traditions must constantly be measured against the scriptures. Metrical and rhymed verses are too limiting for the psalms to speak with their most authentic voice. Various traditional chant forms (Gregorian, Anglican) are still useful, but seldom involve whole congregations except in seminary or monastic settings. One possibility is for cantors or choirs to chant the psalm, while the congregation responds with an antiphon after each line (Psalm 136 apparently is written for that kind of presentation) or each stanza (such as Psalm 46). A slightly different form is used in the Taizé community; the congregation chants a single line over and over, at the same time as a cantor sings through the entire text. I have heard this done, and it can be remarkably beautiful. There is also the Gelineau chant, more rhythmic than Gregorian but less strict than hymn meter. A related form of rhythmic chant is being developed by musicians from the United Methodist Church and the United Church of Canada; an initial presentation of the music, with portions of my translation accented for that system, is available in *Psalms for Singing*, also published by Upper Room.

I am not a musician, and there is little more I could say about different forms of music for psalm singing. But as my translation developed, I received considerable counsel from people who are musicians, and there were two important developments that I should mention.

First, the text is intended to be sung, and was revised more than once in response to musicians' needs. Brevity, rhythm, and clarity were factors that were repeatedly emphasized. By brevity, I mean that I aimed to have no more than four accented syllables, or "beats," in a line. By rhythm, I mean that I sought to reduce the number of unaccented syllables between beats to only one or two. For instance, the phrase "the righteousness of the Lord" has four unaccented syllables in a row and is awkward to read or sing; an equivalent phrase might be "the justice of God," with only two such syllables together. The result is, I have found, a text that is far easier for groups to read aloud, and far easier to set to various types of music. I might add that by clarity I mean that I tried to make my English renderings straightforward and unambiguous, so that musicians would be able to paraphrase if necessary in order to match their melodic lines. One surprising result is that a friend of mine, who is a pastor and who has used earlier drafts of my text, was able to make a very few textual changes—and then to have his congregation sing Psalm 96 to the tune of "Michael, Row Your Boat Ashore"! So the psalm became what many people believe church music should be, a popular "folk" expression in tunes and rhythms familiar from daily life.

Second, I want you to know that my friend is no more a musician than I am; he is simply someone who takes creative worship seriously and is willing to experiment. While I do not feel competent to tell you how to sing the whole Psalter, I urge you to invent for any worship settings in which you are involved—even if you are not a trained musician. You can alternate sections of psalms with verses of hymns (my own most successful experiment is alternating chanted sections of Psalm 32 with verses of "Amazing Grace"). You can learn some of the chant forms (Gregorian and Anglican) that are in the back of at least some denominational hymnals. Because this translation was done with more attention to musicians' suggestions than is usual, it is easier even for nonmusicians to begin to put text and music together.

As soon as we speak of communities at worship, from family devotions to small prayer groups to the full Sunday congregation, we come up against another problem that is not strictly musical, but needs to be discussed here nevertheless. It is the problem of inclusive (sometimes called "non-sexist") language. It is a far more important problem than some people will admit; I know it is important because I see the great impact of male-dominated grammatical norms on the self-esteem of my own daughter. It is also far more complex than some people will admit; our history and tradition provide us with riches that we cannot lightly manipulate in terms of our modern issues without endangering the authenticity of the heritage that we have. I have given much thought to this problem, and need to state some conclusions here, for reasons that will be apparent at the end of this section.

First, there is the matter of "inclusiveness." It is most important that we be truly "inclusive" in dealing with an ancient text that we did not invent and have no authority to modify in any essential way. To eliminate male images for God that are in the text is *not inclusive;* a tyranny of feminine exclusivity is no improvement on our admittedly sorry past. Most translations suppress or gloss over the feminine images for God, in Psalms 2, 90, and 131. Where God is referred to as "mother," or "giving birth," we should say so! But having said so, we need to be equally inclusive when God is called "father" (Psalm 68) or "king" (often!). The fact that the male images outnumber the female is not our business. Nor will mere counting of masculine or feminine images bring any genuine equality. The crucial thing is not numbers of references, but the fact that Israel could imagine God being like a "master" or a "mistress," in successive lines of the same poem (Psalm 123). We need to be as inclusive as they were and allow the text to speak of God as both "masculine" and "feminine."

On the other hand, I see no need to refer to God or to God's people with masculine *or* feminine pronouns. English is so wonderfully flexible that I did not find any line in the psalms which required a gender pronoun to express its meaning—except for Psalm 128 (which is clearly about the blessings offered to *men* in Israel), and of course the psalms that speak of the king of Israel and Judah. Everywhere, I found, we had ways of speaking of God or of God's people which were not ungrammatical, not awkward, not obscure, and not exclusive of either gender.

Some people no doubt will object to the retention of the word "Lord" as the rendering of the divine name Yahweh. I have decided to retain it for three reasons. One is the practical problem of rhythm; such polysyllabic substitutes as "sovereign" would have made the task's complexities even more difficult to manage. The second reason is historical—"Lord" has been the all-but-universal practice of Judaism and Christianity for at least 2,300 years. The third, and decisive, reason is theological. The New Testament's fundamental confession of faith is, "Jesus is Lord" (1 Corinthians 12:3), a confession that not only speaks of Jesus' *office* and authority, but claims that Jesus' *person* manifests the person of the God who is Lord over Israel. Such a connection between Jesus and the God of Israel is not self-evident from the Old Teatament itself; such "royal" Psalms as 2, 72, and 110 were not written about Jesus but about one or another of Israel's historical monarchs. Only *in faith,* by confessing "Jesus is Lord," do we see how Israel's prayers in the Psalter are given God's surprising answer in Jesus Christ. Historic creeds and formulas, then, have very specific meanings, and any attempt at paraphrase may make the formula "relevant" or "understandable" only by perverting its content. (The problem of the Trinity, "Father, Son, and Holy Spirit," is comparable in complexity. I do not see what we can say that is different, yet still says the same things.)

Inclusive language, because it *is* important, will continue to be troublesome. My experience with the psalms suggests that inclusive language for worship texts is possible, but with some historical and doctrinal limits.

The psalms will remain, in the best translation, somewhat archaic and foreign; they do, after all, come from a different language, a different culture, and a different age. (And the preponderance of masculine images for God reflects the time and place of their origin.) Our problem is to be responsive to our own time and its issues, without being false to the psalms themselves, or to the God and the great traditional communities which have given the psalms to us.

The Psalms As Poems

Because the psalms are inevitably archaic and foreign, perhaps some observations about Old Testament poetry, and a few somewhat technical instances of translation difficulties, will help make the psalms more understandable.

The psalms, and other biblical poems as well, are not composed by rhyme, like traditional English verse, nor by strict meter, like classical Greek and Latin poetry. In fact, the poetic nature of much of the Old Testament was completely unrecognized until the eighteenth century, when Robert Lowth, of Oxford, first used the term "parallelism." His basic insight was that Hebrew poems often have pairs of lines in which the second line echoes the first line with different words. Psalm 51 is a good example. So we could speak of Old Testament poetry as a kind of "rhyme of thoughts" instead of sounds. Sometimes the second line states the opposite of the first (Psalm 1, end), or there are sets of three lines (Psalm 1, beginning). But in spite of taking into account these and many other more subtle kinds of "parallelism," many sections of Hebrew poetry have no apparent parallelism at all. We know just how long each line of Psalm 119 is; the lines are arranged in sets of eight, with all the lines in each set beginning with the same letter of the alphabet and all the sets in alphabetical order. But the first section of that psalm alone will show how much variety there can be in the arrangement of ideas. Apparently some kind of rhythm or sentence structure is even more basic than parallelism.

But so far we do not know with any precision just what that rhythm or structure might be.

Still, between the clear parallelism of some sections, and the clear definition of line length in alphabetic psalms (Psalms 37, 111, 112, 145, and others are also alphabetic), we do know more about Hebrew poetry than we once did. And poems in other languages related to Hebrew have clarified many things, so that our knowledge is very much greater just over the last twenty years.

What I have attempted to do in this translation is to match the "feel" of Hebrew rhythms as much as possible. Not necessarily line by line, I hasten to add! Sometimes a very short Hebrew expression demands a fairly long English line. But, in general, lines of three or four beats, with one or two unaccented syllables between beats, are what we find in the psalms.

If I have not always matched the rhythm of particular lines, I have far less often matched their wording. Hebrew is radically different from English, and translators seldom can simply substitute one English word for each Hebrew word and still produce an English sentence. I have done what linguists call "dynamic equivalence" translation— attempting to understand the psalm as a whole, and then saying what each line says in clear and natural English (but briefly, rhythmically, and inclusively!).

At many points, then, this translation differs from the traditional English renderings. Any particular difference could be the result of one (or some combination) of many different factors:

1. A different understanding of a particular line based on the context of the whole psalm;
2. The need to include information obvious to early Israelite hearers, but not likely to be known to modern Christians;
3. A different understanding about the text itself, from comparing the Qumran (Dead Sea) texts, the standard Hebrew text, and the early Greek and Latin translations of the Psalter;

4. New understanding of Hebrew words based on knowledge of other related languages and literatures;
5. Conjectures (hopefully intelligent and informed, not just wild guesses) that are still necessary to make sense of many passages.

Let me give one or two examples of each of these considerations.

1. I have tried to understand each psalm as a whole. The most important breakthrough in biblical study in our time is the fundamental recognition of the different ancient literary types; for the psalms these include hymns, prayers of thanksgiving, royal psalms, wisdom meditations, prayers of personal petition, and communal laments. Each type has its characteristic phrases and tonality, and these need to be taken into account. Very seldom do we have stanzas with refrain (but see Psalm 46, and Psalm 42–43 is shown to be a unity by its refrain), or other structural features we can recognize (except the alphabetic psalms—the alphabetic structure proves that Psalm 9–10 is a unity). But the basic themes are clear, and can be useful translation criteria. In Psalm 118, the psalm as a whole is a song of thanksgiving, a celebration of unexpected victory. The picture one has is the triumphant return of the victorious king at the end of a day of battle. One line in this psalm is often translated:

> This is the day the Lord has made:
> Let us rejoice and be glad in it.

However, the verb "has made" does not need an object in Hebrew, and can be translated, "has acted"; "This day" would then be an adverbial expression of time. And "in it" could just as well be "in him," since Hebrew "day" is masculine (like "God" in Hebrew). Not just to invent ambiguities, but *because of the theme of the whole psalm,* I therefore translate:

> This very day the Lord has acted;
> Let us shout and rejoice in God.

2. Psalm 101 was almost surely spoken by or on behalf of the king. No one else has the authority or responsibility expressed in this poem. So I have made explicit reference to "king" and "royal" household, because I think the original hearers would automatically have had that information even though the Hebrew text only implies it. And in Psalm 24, a pre-Israelite text from ancient Ugarit (a Canaanite city in Syria) has made the image of the "gates" much clearer. "Lifting up" the gates does not refer to opening them; the picture is of the gate towers of Jerusalem seated in a circle and slumped over in despair, until the word comes that the Lord is victorious. Then they are called to stand up straight to receive their returning hero, God. So I have added "despondent," which is not in the Hebrew, because I wanted the image to be the same for modern people as it was for the ancients who knew the metaphor.

Actually, the figure of speech in the Canaanite text was not a circle of towers but the council of the gods. The Israelite poet used the image but substituted Jerusalem's gate towers for the circle of pagan (that is, false) gods. This brings me to another point. Sometimes the Israelites denied that pagan gods had any real existence at all (Isaiah 46:5-7). But often in the psalms (such as Psalm 47) the reality of pagan gods is not denied—instead, they are commanded to submit to the Lord. Sometimes natural forces are regarded as divine beings who operate under God's direction; therefore, I have capitalized Dawn and Dusk in Psalm 75. And sometimes the pagan gods are seen as immortal beings who have rebelled against the God of Israel (Psalm 58); the gods are real and dangerous, but they are still subject to God's judgment. The New Testament calls them "principalities and powers" (Romans 8:38) or "elemental spirits" (Colossians 2:8). Discoveries of ancient pagan texts have shown us a great deal about these pagan gods, and have shown as well the variety of ways in which Israelite and Christian writers have dealt with them.

3. Psalm 122 has "the assembly of Israel" rather than "a command for Israel"; the Psalms scroll from Cave 11 at

Qumran has my reading, while the traditional reading probably was influenced by a similar phrase in Psalm 81. And in Psalm 145 I have restored one verse that is in the early Greek translation, but was accidentally omitted in the Hebrew manuscripts. This is a clear instance where the Greek is correct, for Psalm 145 is alphabetic, and the missing line is the "N" line.

4. In Psalm 29 I originally translated one line "In the temple *declare* God's glory." I am now persuaded that this is a very ancient psalm. In the texts from Ugarit, the word that means "say" or "speak" in Hebrew has the meaning "see." I would read the verb as passive, and now translate: "In the temple God's glory *appears*."

5. In many places in the psalms, all these other resources fail us and we must still rely on imagination to reconstruct or translate the text. Most of the conjectures involved in my translation came from the publications of other scholars. One of the few that did not is in Psalm 46: "The mountains topple *into the valleys*." The Hebrew word behind the last phrase is very similar to the standard Hebrew text "in pride." In a few other places I have bracketed lines that seem to be secondary additions (the end of Psalms 41, 51, and others), or omitted elements that are not part of the psalm text itself (especially the psalm titles and musical instructions—still so very poorly understood).

One final point. Hebrew students have known some things for generations that have been unforgivably withheld from current translations. Perhaps the reason has been that we Christians want to continue to think of the Jews as "legalistic" (which they never were); perhaps it is because Protestants have dominated biblical scholarship until recently, and we are excessively given to moralism (in fact we are more "pharisaical" than the Pharisees ever were!). The Hebrew word "Torah" does not mean "Law"; it means "teaching" or "instruction." Nowhere in my translation will the word "Law" be found. In addition, I have tried to reduce legalistic terminology—like "statute" and "ordinance," in favor of more personal terms like "command," "order," and "direction." The difference is important; God does tell us what to do—but in person, not by citing the paragraphs of some municipal code! The Torah was not a constitution, but a teaching instrument, a way of coming to *understand* justice and right, so that one would know what to do even in the unprecedented situation. I have also used words like "justice" and "oppression" more often than "righteousness" or "evil." Truth and right in Israel were not only personal rather than statutory; they were social rather than individual. You couldn't be "good" in any real sense unless you were good *for* something, good for the community. And "evil people," "sinners," were those who disrupted the community—exploiting the helpless, perverting justice, corrupting corporate worship.

By no means have I written all that the psalms, or the community of scholars, or the fellowship of the church, have taught me. But you are far more likely to learn from the psalms themselves than you are to learn from me. Pray them with all your heart and soul and strength! And may God answer your prayer, as my prayers have been answered in Christ—beyond not only what I deserved, but what I ever hoped or dreamed.

PSALM 1

Happy are those who reject evil counsel,
   Who do not approve of the conduct of sinners,
     Who do not sit among those who mock God.
Instead, the Lord's teaching so delights them
   They ponder it day and night,
     Becoming like trees transplanted near water.
They bear fruit in season;
   Their leaves do not wither,
     And all that they do turns out well.

Not so the guilty!
   They are like wind-scattered husks.
They will not last through the judgment;
   The righteous assembly will not include sinners.
The Lord approves of the deeds of the just,
   But an evil life leads only to ruin.

PSALM 2

Why do the nations conspire,
   The peoples grumble in vain,
The kings of the world take a stand,
   And the tyrants assemble together
     Against the Lord's anointed king?

"Let us tear off his bonds,
   And hurl from ourselves his reins!"
Enthroned in the sky, God laughs;
   The Lord scornfully mocks them—
Then speaks to them in wrath
   And terrifying anger:
"I have anointed my king,

On Zion, my holy mountain,
   I, God, declare my decree."

The Lord said to me, "You are my son;
   Today I give birth to you.
Ask me—I give you the nations;
   The world's farthest regions are yours.
With an iron staff you will break them;
   You will smash them like jars of clay."

And now, you kings, pay attention;
   Earth's rulers, listen to reason.
Serve the Lord in fear,
   And kiss God's feet in terror.
God's anger, so easily kindled,
   Will make you wandering beggars.
      But all who trust in the Lord will be blessed.

PSALM 3

Lord, how many oppressors I have!
   How many rise up against me!
How many are those who say to me,
   "God will not come to save you."

Yet you shield me, Lord, on every side.
   You are my glory; you lift up my head.
I cry aloud to you, Lord;
   From your holy mountain you answer.

I can lie down and sleep;
   I awake, for the Lord sustains me.
I will not fear ten thousand people
   Who attack me from every side.

Get up, Lord;
   Save me, my God!
You batter the jaws of all my foes;
   You break the teeth of the wicked.
O Lord, you are salvation;
   Your blessing rests on your people.

PSALM 4

Answer me, God, when I call;
　It is you who find me not guilty.
Give me room to resist my accuser;
　Hear my prayer with compassion.
People, how long will you scorn me,
　Loving vanity, seeking deception?
Know that God honors fidelity;
　The Lord hears me when I call.
Tremble with fear, lest you sin;
　Ponder and grieve on your beds.
Worship God with appropriate sacrifice,
　And put your trust in the Lord.
Many people are saying,
　"Who can give us anything good?
Let the light of your presence, Lord,
　Arise to shine upon us."
You give me greater joy
　Than all their food and drink.
In utter peace I lie down to sleep;
　My life is safe in you alone.

PSALM 5

Hear what I say, O Lord;
　Notice my sighs.
Attend to the sound of my cry for help,
　My King and my God.
For I pray to you, O Lord;
　Each morning, hear my voice.
Each morning, I ready myself for you,
　And wait in expectation.
For you are no God who delights in evil;
　You harbor nothing harmful.
Self-deceivers cannot stand firm
　And look you in the eye.
You hate all those who do wrong;
　You exterminate those who tell lies.

Those who betray and murder
  Are abominable to the Lord.
But because you are so gracious,
  I will go to your house.
I bow down at your holy temple,
  And there I worship you.
Guide me in your justice, Lord,
  Because of my enemies.
Make your ways plain before me,
  For nothing real comes from their mouths.
Their inner lives are in ruins;
  Their tongues are smooth,
    Their gullets an open grave.
Condemn them, O God;
  Let their schemes be their downfall!
Banish them for their many crimes,
  For they are stubborn against you.
And all who seek refuge in you will rejoice;
  They will shout in eternal joy.
And those who adore your name
  Will exult in you, their defender.
For you will bless the righteous, Lord,
  Your favor surrounding them like a shield.

PSALM 6

Do not reprove me, Lord, in anger,
  Nor discipline me in your wrath.
Be gracious to me; I am frail.
  Heal my terrified frame.
I even fear for my life—
  Lord, how long must I wait for you?
Turn back, Lord; save my life.
  Show your mercy and rescue me.
For the dead do not remember you—
  Who praises you from the grave?
I am so weary from groaning!
  I weep all night;
I drench my bed;

I dissolve my couch in tears.
My eyes are bleary and sore;
  I am worn out by so many foes!

Away from me, all who do harm,
  For the Lord has heard my weeping.
The Lord has heard my call for help;
  The Lord has accepted my prayer.
Oh, the terror and shame of all my foes—
  Turned back in sudden humiliation!

PSALM 7

O Lord my God, I take refuge in you;
  Rescue and save me from all who pursue me,
Lest they prey on me like lions,
  Tearing my throat while I am helpless.

My Lord God, if I have done what they say,
  If in fact my hands are guilty,
If I have harmed my friend
  And falsely aided those who oppress us,
Let the enemy hunt me down
  And trample my life to the ground,
    Leaving my honor to lie in the dust.

Arise, O Lord, in your anger;
  Bear my oppressor away in rage.
Awake, and do justice on my behalf;
  Let the Lord judge the peoples!
The council of nations surrounds you;
  Return from heaven before their eyes.
Judge me, for I am righteous;
  My Exalted Lord, I am blameless!
Do harm to those who are evil,
  And make the righteous secure.
It is you who test hearts and minds,
  O righteous God!

The exalted God is my sovereign,
  The savior of all who want what is right.

God vindicates the righteous,
  Passing sentence all day long.
Returning in triumph, with sharpened sword,
  God draws a bow and aims the arrow;
The tools of death are God's to use,
  God who produces arrows of fire!
"Here are people pregnant with evil,
  Conceiving distress, giving birth to lies.
Let them dig their pits and prepare them;
  They will fall into traps they made themselves.
Their distress will come back on their own heads,
  Their violence descend on their own skulls!"
Let me praise the Lord, who is just,
  And sing the name of God Most High.

PSALM 8

  Lord, our Lord, how splendid is your name in all the
    world!
I will worship your grandeur above the skies,
  Though I babble like infants and children;
You have built a fortress against your opponents,
  To stop the avenging foes.
When I look at the sky, the work of your fingers,
  The moon and stars you secured in place,
Why do you consider mere mortals,
  Attending to us, who are only human?
You make us lack little compared with yourself!
  You crown us with glory and grandeur.
You make us rule your other creatures;
  You put everything under our feet—
All sheep and cattle,
  And even wild creatures,
The birds of the sky and the fish of the sea,
  Whatever traverses the paths of the sea.
    Lord, our Lord, how splendid is your name in all the
      world!

PSALMS 9 and 10

I will praise you, Lord, with all my heart;
  I will recite all your marvelous deeds.
I will rejoice and exult in you,
  And sing to your name, O God Most High,
While my foes retreat before you;
  They flee, in stumbling confusion.
For you do justice on my behalf;
  You sit on your throne as righteous judge.
You rebuke the nations, destroying the wicked;
  You blot out their names forever and ever.
You uproot their cities, whose names are forgotten;
  Their ruins lie silent forevermore.
But you, O Lord, are sovereign forever,
  Your throne of judgment is secure.
And you will justly rule the world,
  Rightly redressing wrongs among nations.
May you be a tower for all who are crushed,
  A high tower in distressing times.
That those who know your nature may trust you,
  For you never abandon any who seek you.

Sing to the Lord, enthroned on Zion;
  Recite to the nations God's wonderful deeds.
For God takes vengeance when blood is shed;
  God never forgets the cry of the poor.

See, gracious God, how their hatred afflicts me;
  It is you who must pick me up from death's door,
That I may go on reciting your praise,
  And sing in Jerusalem's gate how you saved me.
The nations sink down in the pit they have made;
  Their own feet are caught in the net they concealed.
In doing justice the Lord is revealed;
  In the things they contrive the wicked are snared.
Let the wicked return to the world of the dead,
  All these nations forgetful of God.
For the needy will not be forgotten forever,
  Nor the hopes of the poor be long disappointed.
Arise, O Lord! Let no mortal defy you!

Let the nations be judged in your very presence!
Put the fear of the Lord in them;
    Let the peoples know they are mortal and frail!
Why, O Lord, do you stay far away,
    Averting your gaze in distressing times?
With fierce pride the wicked pursue the poor.
    Let them be caught in their own precious schemes.
For the wicked worship their own desires;
    They kneel before the god of greed.
The wicked dismiss the Lord with scorn;
    "No divine wrath will seek us out."
So convinced are they that there is no God,
    They constantly profane God's ways.
Your judgments, Lord, are too lofty for them;
    In all their designs they disdain your decrees.
They assure themselves, "We will never stumble!"
    "Pleasure with no misgivings!" they vow.
They speak of nothing but fraud and extortion;
    Their tongues talk of wretched deeds of deceit.
They sit in ambush within the courtyards;
    From hidden places they murder the innocent.
Furtively watching for someone defenseless,
    Crouched like lions concealed in a thicket,
They lie in wait to seize the poor,
    To seize the poor whom their nets entangle.
The righteous are crushed and thrown down;
    The defenseless fall into their clutches.
So the wicked tell themselves, "God has forgotten;
    God turns away, and will never notice."
Get up, Lord God, and use your power!
    Do not forget the poor!
Why are the guilty so arrogant, Lord?
    They think you will not pursue them!
Can't you see? It is you who distress us!
    Look at us, and give us your help!
The defenseless are forced to depend on you;
    It is you who must save the orphans.
Break the arm of the guilty oppressors;
    Search out their guilt—or can't you find it?
Rule, O Lord, forever and ever,

Make the nations disperse from your land.
Heed, O Lord, the hopes of the poor;
   Strengthen their will and hear them.
Provide justice for orphans and victims;
   And banish fear from this land!

PSALM 11

I trust in the Lord; how can you people say,
   "Flee, little bird, to your mountaintop!
Look! The wicked are drawing their bows;
   They carefully aim their arrows,
      To shoot from the shadows at those who are upright.
Look! Everything is falling to pieces!
   The righteous are left defenseless!"

But the Lord resides in the holy temple;
   The Lord is enthroned above the skies.
The eyes of God peer down and examine
   All the descendants of Adam.
The Lord examines the just and the wicked,
   And hates those who love to be cruel.
God pours on the wicked sulfurous fire,
   And then, to cool them—a whirlwind!
The Lord is just, and loves deeds of justice;
   Those who do right will behold God's face.

PSALM 12

Save us, Lord! No one cares anymore;
   Trust has gone from the human race.
They all speak deceit to their neighbors,
   With flattering lips and double meanings.
The Lord will cut off their flattering lips,
   Their tongues that talk so boldly—
They say, "Our tongues will make us mighty;
   Our lips are our allies, no one can rule us."

"The helpless poor groan from their wounds,
　　But now I arise!" says the Lord.
　　　"I bring salvation to all who pant for it."
The Lord's declarations are pure,
　　Silver refined in a furnace,
　　　Seven times cleansed from every impurity.

You, eternal Lord, must protect us;
　　You have guarded us since ancient times.
On every side the wicked are prowling,
　　Scornful and haughty toward all other people.

PSALM 13

How long, Lord? Will you always forget me?
　　How long will you hide your face from me?
How long must I scheme just to survive,
　　My mind in anguish day after day?
　　　How long will my enemy rise against me?

Look at me, answer me, Lord my God;
　　Give light to my eyes, lest I sleep in death,
Lest my enemy say, "I have triumphed";
　　My oppressors shriek for joy as I fall.
I have trusted in your fidelity;
　　The joy of my heart is your salvation.
　　　I sing to the Lord, who brings me through.

PSALM 14

Fools convince themselves
　　That there is no God.
Their every action corrupts and destroys;
　　Not one does what is good.
The Lord looks down from the sky,
　　At all the descendants of Adam,
To see if anyone is wise,
　　If anyone seeks for God.

But everyone has deserted,
  Corrupted altogether;
Not one does what is good,
  Not a single one!

Don't you know, you who do wrong—
  You who devour my people for food—
    Won't they cry to the Lord?
They were terribly afraid,
  But the Lord is among the righteous.
You have ruined the plans of the poor,
  But the Lord is their refuge.

Who will bring from the Mount of Zion
  Salvation for Israel?
When the Lord brings back the exiles,
  God's people, Jacob, will celebrate;
    Israel will shout for joy.

PSALM 15

Lord, who is a guest in your home?
  Who lives on your holy mountain?

One whose conduct is blameless,
  Whose actions are just,
    And whose will is to speak the truth;
Whose tongue slanders no one,
  Who wrongs no neighbor,
    Who treats no friend with disrespect;
Who hates the sight of despicable people,
  But who honors those who fear God,
    Who accuses the lawless and does not relent;
Who accepts neither interest on loans,
  Nor bribes against the innocent;
    One who acts in these ways never stumbles.

PSALM 16

Protect me, O God; I seek refuge in you,
  Saying, "Lord, you are my Lord;

Does not all my good come from you?"
But as for the world's "holy gods,"
  So splendid to those who find joy in them,
    How those who pursue them increase their own
    troubles!
I pour out to them no libations of blood,
  Nor take their names upon my lips.
The Lord is the one who feeds me;
  O God, you are my provider.
You apportion fine things to me;
  What you have allotted, delights me.
I bless the Lord, who counsels me;
  Even my sleepless nights instruct me.
I am always aware of your presence;
  When you hold me, I cannot fall.
My heart rejoices and sings,
  And even my flesh is kept secure.
For you will not leave me to die,
  Nor give to the grave your faithful one.
You will show me the path to life,
  And the utter delight of your presence;
    In your right hand are the joys that endure.

PSALM 17

Hear, righteous Lord; attend to my cry!
  Listen to me as I pray without falsehood.
May you declare me innocent;
  May you discern my integrity.
You have tested my will;
  You have visited me in the night.
You have refined me with fire—
  Have you not found out my plans?
I have no praise for human deeds;
  In the words of your lips I am secure.
I hold my steps to the way you command;
  In your paths my feet will not stumble.
I call you, God, for you answer me.
  Turn your ear to me; hear my word.
Surprise your saints with your saving power;

We are safe from attack in your right hand.
Guard me as you guard your own eye,
  And shelter me under your wings,
From the evil ones who assault me,
  From my mortal foes who surround me.
They are fat and gross, with haughty words,
  Prowling around us to bring us down.
They are like lions, eager for prey;
  Like young lions, lying in ambush.
Rise up, God; confront them, and make them bow down.
  Let your sword save my life from their evil.
Destroy them, Lord; let your hand destroy them,
  In spite of their wealth, in the prime of their life.
But fill the stomachs of those whom you cherish;
  May their children survive to inherit their wealth.
When justice is done, I will see your face,
  Fulfilled, when I wake, by the vision of you.

PSALM 18

I love you, O Lord, my strength;
  Lord, my rock, my fortress, my savior.
In God, my rock, I seek safety,
  My shield, my strong helper, my refuge.
I cry to the Lord, who is worthy of praise,
  And I am saved from my foes.

The waves of death were all around me,
  The floods of destruction terrified me.
The bonds of Hades were looped about me,
  The snares of imminent death.
In my peril I cried out, "Lord!"
  I called for help to my God.
From your palace you heard my cry;
  My call for help came to your ears.
An earthquake shook the world;
  There were shudders beneath the mountains;
    They shook because God was angry.
From God's nostrils, smoke ascended;

From God's mouth came devouring fire,
   God spewed out flaming coals.
God opened the sky, and came down,
   Standing upon a storm-cloud,
Borne on the flying cherubim,
   Swooping on wings of wind!
Enclosed in darkness all around,
   Sheltered within the storm of rain,
The light of God's presence propelled the clouds,
   With hail and bolts of lightning.
The Lord thundered and stormed from the sky,
   The High God shouted aloud.
God fired arrows that scattered them all;
   They fled from the lightning in panic.
The beds of seas were exposed,
   The foundations of earth revealed,
By your mighty blast, O Lord,
   By the stormy breath of your nostrils.
God reached down to grasp me,
   To draw me out of deep waters.
God saved me from mighty enemies;
   From foes who outnumbered me.
They attacked me on that disastrous day,
   But the Lord was the staff that upheld me.
God brought me out to an open place,
   And was happy to rescue me.
The Lord rewarded my innocence,
   Repaying my hands that did no wrong.
For I have kept the ways of the Lord,
   I have never rebelled against my God.
I am always aware of your judgment;
   I will not deviate from your orders.
I have been completely devoted to you,
   And kept myself from offending you.
You, Lord, repaid my innocence,
   For you know my hands did no wrong.
You are loyal to those who are loyal,
   And devoted to all those devoted to you.
You are honest with those who are honest,
   But you will outwit the crafty!

You rescue the lowly people,
    But lay low those who are haughty.
You are my shining lamp, O Lord,
    Illuminating my darkness.
With you, I stride over canyons;
    With my God, I leap any wall.
How perfect the way of God!
        The word of the Lord—how pure!
            You protect everyone who trusts you.
For who can be God, except the Lord?
    Who is our rock, aside from our God?
The God whose power holds me fast,
    Whose might can make me completely free;
The God who makes me run like a deer,
    And sets me upon the high places.
It is God who instructs my hands for war,
    My arm for bending a bow of bronze.
You give to me your protecting shield,
    While your right hand supports me,
        And your help makes me great.
Traversing the land with great strides,
    My ankles are firm and strong.
I pursue my foes, and overtake them,
    And never turn back until they are destroyed.
        They fall beneath my feet.
You made me strong for the battle;
    You compelled the rebels to kneel at my feet,
Their heads to the ground, their necks exposed,
    And I silenced all who hated me.
They cried for help, but no one saved them;
    They called you, Lord, but you would not answer.
I grind them down like dust on the road;
    I pulverize them like dirt in the street.
You saved me from contentious people,
    And set me above the nations.
People I never knew will serve me;
    The foreigners will cringe before me.
        As soon as they hear, they obey!
The foreigners wither in terror,
    And crawl to me out of their strongholds.

The Lord lives! Let my rock be blessed;
  My savior and God be raised high!
Is it not God who gave me revenge,
  And subjected the nations to me?
You deliver me from my enemies;
  You lift me above my foes;
    You save me from violent people.
So I praise you among the nations,
  And I sing out your name, O Lord;
You have given your king such triumph,
  In faithfulness to your anointed—
    To David and his endless line.

PSALM 19

The skies are declaring God's glory,
  The firmament tells of the work of God's hands.
Day bubbles forth speech to day,
  And night proclaims knowledge to night;
Without speech, without words—
  Their voice is not heard—
Their call goes out to all places,
  And their news to the ends of the world.

There God pitched a tent for the sun—
  Like a bridegroom leaving his chamber,
    Like a hero eager to run a race,
The sun comes from the end of the skies,
  And goes round to their farthest limits,
    And nothing can hide from its heat.

The Lord's instruction is perfect,
  Renewing life.
The Lord's command can be trusted,
  Making simple folk wise.
The Lord's directions are true;
  They gladden the mind.
The Lord's decree is bright,
  Giving light to the eyes.

The fear of the Lord is pure;
  It stands forever.
The Lord's verdicts are right;
  They are utterly just.
Are they not more precious than gold,
  Than much fine gold?
And are they not sweeter than honey,
  Than honey in combs?
Indeed your servant takes warning from them;
  There is great reward in keeping them.
Can anyone see their own errors?
  Keep me free from secrets!
In humility let me serve you;
  Do not let my pride govern me!
Then I shall be blameless,
  And free from any great wrong.

May you be pleased by the words of my mouth;
  May you be in my mind's meditations,
    O Lord, my rock and redeemer.

PSALM 20

In your day of distress, may the Lord answer you;
  May the name of Jacob's God protect you.
May God send you help from the holy place,
  And strengthen you from Zion.
May God recall all your offerings,
  Accepting this your sacrifice.
May God give to you your heart's desire,
  Causing all your plans to succeed.
May we shout for joy at your victory,
  And raise in triumph the name of our God.
    May the Lord fulfill all that you ask!

"And now I know that you, O Lord,
  Will rescue me, your anointed king!
From your holy skies you answer me,
  And save me by your right hand's power."

Some trust in chariots, some in horses,
  But we will swear by the Lord our God.
Others will collapse and surrender;
  But we will arise, and sustain one another.
O Lord, grant victory to the king;
  Answer us on the day that we call you.

PSALM 21

Lord, in your strength the king rejoices,
  In your salvation he shouts for joy!
You give to him his heart's desire;
  The request of his lips you have not denied.
For you bring to him good blessings,
  You have set on his head a wreath of gold.
Life he asks; you give it to him;
  Length of days forever and always.
Great is his glory by your saving power;
  You bestow on him majestic splendor—
For you have given him blessings for ever;
  You gladden him with joy in your presence.
For the king trusts in the Most High God;
  In the Lord's loyalty he does not stumble.
Your hand will search out all your foes;
  Your right hand will reach all those who hate you.
You will make them like a fiery furnace
  At the time you appear, O Lord.
Their offspring will perish from the world,
  Their seed from among the people.
For they planned evil schemes against you.
  But their intrigues will not succeed,
For you will turn them to flight;
  With your bow you take aim at their face.
Rise up, O Lord, in your strength;
  Let us sing and praise your power.

PSALM 22

My God, my God, why abandon me?
  My groaning words do not help me at all!
All day I call, but you do not answer;
  All night, but I find no rest.
And yet, my God, you are holy,
  Enthroned on Israel's praises.
Our ancestors put their faith in you;
  They had faith, and you rescued them.
They cried out to you and were saved;
  They had faith, and you did not shame them.
But I am a worm, not human at all;
  A disgrace to everyone, scorned by the people.
And all who see me mock me—
  Making faces and shaking their heads:
"You trust in the Lord—let the Lord come to help you;
  Let God be your savior, if God is your friend!"
It was you who drew me out of the womb,
  Who kept me safe on my mother's breast.
I was thrown on you from birth;
  From my mother's womb you have been my God.
Do not be far away from me!
  For trouble is near; there is no one to help.
So many bulls encircle me;
  Mighty bulls of Bashan surround me.
They open their mouths against me—
  They are tearing, roaring lions.
I am poured out like water,
  And all my joints torn apart;
My courage is melted wax,
  My strength, a crumbling pot.
My tongue sticks to the roof of my mouth;
  You prepare me for dusty death.
For savage dogs surround me,
  An evil horde besieges me.
From head to foot, every bone hurts,
  And everyone stares at me.
They apportion my clothes among them;
  They throw their dice for my robe.

O Lord, do not be far away;
　　Hurry to help me, for you are my strength!
Keep my body safe from the sword,
　　My mortal frame from the ax's edge;
Rescue me from the lion's mouth,
　　My humble self from the wild bull's horns.

I declare your name to my brothers and sisters;
　　In the congregation I praise you:
"All who worship the Lord,
　　Every descendant of Jacob,
All of Israel's offspring,
　　Now honor and fear your God!
For God will not ignore the poor,
　　Nor despise them because they are wretched.
God's face is not hidden from them;
　　God hears their cry for help."
In the great assembly I praise you;
　　Fulfilling my vows among those who fear you.
The poor will eat and be filled;
　　The seekers will praise the Lord.
The world will remember and turn to the Lord;
　　Every nation and clan will bow down.
For the Lord alone will reign;
　　God rules among the nations.
Even the dead will bow down to the Lord,
　　And those who are dust will kneel before God.
And when my life has come to an end,
　　My offspring will serve the Lord.
Declare God's justice to future ages;
　　Tell those yet unborn, what the Lord has done!

PSALM 23

Lord, my shepherd, there's nothing I lack.
　　In fresh pastures you let me lie down;
You lead me beside quiet waters;
　　You restore me to life.

In order to show who you are,
  You guide me in paths that are right.
Even walking through dark valleys,
  I have no fear of harm.
For you yourself are with me;
  Your rod and staff reassure me.

Right in front of my foes,
  You lay out a feast for me.
You anoint my head with oil;
  My cup is overflowing.

Goodness and love pursue me
  Every day of my life;
God's house will be my home
  As long as I may live.

PSALM 24

The earth and its fullness belong to the Lord,
  The world and all its inhabitants.
God laid its foundations upon the seas;
  Over cosmic rivers God made it stand firm.
Who can go up to the Lord's own mountain?
  Who can stand in God's holy place?
Those whose hands have done no wrong,
  And those whose motives are pure;
Who do not live by deceit,
  Or take oaths intending to break them.
They will receive the Lord's blessing;
  Their savior God will declare them guiltless.
Their whole generation will search for you,
  And seek your presence, O God of Jacob.

Lift up your heads, despondent gates;
  You ancient towers, stand tall!
    The glorious king is coming.
Who is this glorious king?
  The Lord, with heroic strength;
    The Lord, heroic in war.

Lift up your heads, despondent gates;
   You ancient towers, stand tall!
      The glorious king is coming.
Who is this glorious king?
   The Lord of the armies of earth and sky—
      God is the glorious king.

PSALM 25

To you, O Lord, I give my life;
   You are my God.
I trust you; you will not shame me;
   Do not let my enemies gloat at my downfall!
Do not disappoint those who wait for you,
   But let the treacherous come to grief.
Make me know your paths, O Lord;
   And teach me your ways.
Teach me to walk by faith in you,
   For you are the God who saves me.
I wait for you eagerly all day long,
   Because of your goodness, O Lord.
Remember your mercy and gracious love—
   The qualities you have always had.
Forget my youthful rebellions and sins;
   Remember me as one whom you love.
The Lord is just and good,
   And teaches sinners the way,
Guiding humble people to justice,
   And showing them how to find it.
Lord, act with eternal kindness
   Toward those who keep your covenant.
For the sake of your name, O Lord,
   Forgive my sin, great as it is.
Will you not teach your chosen way
   To all who worship you?
Let them sleep knowing all is well;
   Let their children possess the world.
O Lord, counsel those who fear you,
   And teach them your covenant.

My eyes always look to you, Lord;
  Disentangle my feet from the net!
Turn to me, and be gracious,
  For I am poor and alone.
Open my mind in times of distress;
  Direct me out of my troubles.
See how I toil in misery,
  And take away all my sin.
See how my foes multiply,
  How they hate me with violent hatred.
Save my life! Rescue me!
  I find shelter in you; do not shame me.
Let perfect integrity guard me,
  For I am waiting for you.
God will redeem Israel
  From every kind of oppression.

PSALM 26

Judge me, O Lord, for I walk the true way,
  And I trust that in you I will not be unsteady.
Lord, put me to the test and try me;
  Refine my heart and mind with fire.
For I look to your steadfast care for me,
  And act out of confidence in you.
I do not sit with worthless people,
  Nor walk with those who pretend to be good.
I hate the company of the malicious,
  And will not associate with oppressors.
In innocence I wash my hands,
  And worship at your altar, Lord.
I make your praise heard with my voice,
  Reciting all your marvelous acts.
Lord, I love the house where you live,
  The place where your glory resides.
Do not kill me along with sinners,
  Nor with murderers condemn me to die—
With those whose left hand hides a knife,
  While the right hand takes a bribe.

For I have walked with integrity;
  Redeem me and show me your kindness.
As long as I can stand firm,
  I will bless you, Lord, among your people.

PSALM 27

The Lord is my light and my freedom;
  Who shall make me afraid?
The Lord defends my life;
  Who can terrify me?
When the evil come to devour my flesh—
  My oppressors and foes—they stumble and fall.
If they pitch camp against me,
  I will still be confident.
I ask one thing from the Lord,
  And I will seek it—
To live in the Lord's house
  All my life long;
To contemplate the Lord's beauty,
  To begin the day in God's temple.
For you shield me within your temple
  On a day of evil;
You will hide me within your sheltering tent,
  Or lift me high upon a rock,
So that my head is lifted high
  Before the foes that surround me.
I will joyfully sacrifice at your tent;
  I will sing and play music to you, O Lord.
"Hear my voice, Lord," I cry out.
  "Be gracious and answer me."
"Come," I say to myself;
  "Seek God's presence."
Lord, I do seek your presence;
  Do not hide your face from me.
Do not dismiss your servant in anger;
  You are my helper.
Do not abandon or leave me;
  You are my savior God.

Though my parents abandon me,
  The Lord will embrace me.
Lord, teach me your ways;
  Lead me in right paths, in spite of my foes.
Do not put me into my enemies' power;
  Malicious perjurors rise up against me.
Shall I not live to see the Lord's goodness?
  Wait for the Lord; take courage!
God will strengthen your will.
  Wait for the Lord.

PSALM 28

Don't be deaf when I call you, Lord!
  Your silence is deadly to me!
Hear when I cry to you for help,
  When I reach out toward your temple.
Don't drag me off with the guilty,
  With those who harm others,
With those who speak peace to their neighbors,
  But have evil plans in their hearts.
Deal with them in accord with their acts,
  In accord with their cruel deeds;
Pay them back for what they have done—
  Turn their schemes against them.
Because they ignore what you have done,
  May you tear them down, and never rebuild them!

Bless the Lord, who has heard my plea;
  My heart trusts in the Lord, my strength and shield.
God helps me, renewing my courage;
  I will praise God with my song.
Lord, you are your people's strength;
  You are the king's saving fortress.
Save and bless your special people,
  Shepherd and carry them always.

PSALM 29

Give to the Lord, you creatures of heaven,
  Give to the Lord all glory and power.
Give to the Lord a glorious name;
  Bow down to the Lord in holy splendor.

The voice of the Lord sounds over the oceans—
  Crashing thunder above the deep seas.
The voice of the Lord is power;
  The voice of the Lord is splendor.
The voice of the Lord splits the cedars;
  God splinters the cedars of Lebanon.
God makes Lebanon skip like a calf,
  Mount Hermon skip like a wild young ox.

Slashing the sky with lightning-swords,
  The Lord's voice makes the desert writhe;
    The desert of Kadesh quakes.
In terror, the deer flee God's thunder,
  That snaps the limbs from the trees;
    In the temple God's glory appears!

The throne of the Lord is above sky and sea;
  The Lord will rule forever.
Lord, give strength to your people;
  Lord, bless your people with peace.

PSALM 30

Lord, I exalt you, for you lift me up,
  And keep my foes from rejoicing over me.
My God, I cry to you for help,
  It is you who heal me, Lord.
You brought me up from the grave;
  You restored me to life from among the dead.

Let faithful people sing to the Lord;
  Let them praise the holy God,
Whose anger is brief, whose grace is lifelong—
  We weep in the evening, but laugh at dawn.

I, unconcerned, said to myself,
  "I will never stumble."
You allowed me to stand like a splendid mountain;
  But you hid your face, and I was in terror.

I cried out to you, Lord;
  I sought my Lord's mercy—
"What will you gain if I die in tears?
  Does dust declare your faithful love?"

Lord, you heard, and were gracious to me;
  O Lord, you were my helper.
You turned my grief into dancing,
  Stripped me of sorrow and clothed me with joy.
So my heart will sing to you, not weep;
  Lord, my God, I will praise you forever.

PSALM 31

Lord, I seek refuge in you;
  Do not shame me, eternal God.
Rescue me, in accord with your justice;
  Hear me, and hurry to save me.
Be for me a mountain stronghold,
  A high, inaccessible shelter.
For you are my rocky stronghold;
  Guide me and lead me as only you can.
You, my fortress, bring me out
  From the net they have set to trap me.
Into your hand I commit my spirit;
  Faithful Lord God, redeem me.
I hate those who care about vanities;
  I will trust in the Lord.
I shout aloud for joy,
  And delight in your constant love.
In love, you saw my sorrow,
  And knew my inner distress;
You kept me out of my enemy's clutches,
  And gave me a broad place to stand.
Be gracious, Lord, for I have an oppressor;
  My inmost self is dissolved in grief.

My life is ending in torment;
  My years are gone with a sigh.
My sin has shaken my strength,
  And my bones dissolve in weakness.
All my oppressors torment me;
  Even worse, so do my neighbors!
My friends are afraid to know me;
  When we meet on the street, they flee.
They forget me as though I had died,
  Like a tool that is lost or broken.
I hear all their lying rumors—
  And I am enveloped in fear—
How they conspire against me,
  Plotting to take my life!
But Lord, I will trust in you;
  I say, "You are my God."
My times are in your hands;
  Save me from hostile pursuers.
Let your face shine on your servant;
  Let your fidelity save me.
Lord, do not shame me; I call to you!
  Let the guilty die in shame!
Silence their lying lips,
  Their brazen contempt for the righteous.

How great is the goodness you have in store
  For those who worship you!
All humanity sees what you offer
  To those who seek refuge in you.
You hide them in your secret presence
  From every human slander,
Concealing them in your shelter
  From every accusing tongue.

Bless the Lord whose marvelous love
  Is mine in this mighty city!
Dismayed, I thought I was cut off from you,
  But you heard my plea when I cried to you.

Love the Lord, all you faithful people.
  The Lord defends those who are steadfast,
    And more than repays the proud!

Be strong, persist in your purpose,
    All you who wait for the Lord.

PSALM 32

Happy are those whose offense is pardoned,
    Whose sin is forgiven;
Whom the Lord considers not guilty,
    In whose spirit is no deceit.

When I kept silent, my bones were exhausted,
    Because I was groaning all day long.
Day and night your hand weighed me down;
    Great God, you were like a scorching drought.
But when I told you my sin,
    No longer concealing my guilt,
I confessed my offense to you,
    And Lord, you forgave my sin.

So your saints in need pray to you,
    And the torrents never reach them.
You hide me, to save me from the oppressor;
    You surround me, to bring me to safety:
"I show you and teach you the way you should go;
    I counsel you, watching over you."

Do not be stupid like horses or mules,
    Their temper restrained by muzzle and bridle.
The pains of transgressors are many,
    But love surrounds those who trust in the Lord.
Sing joyfully, you who are right with God;
    Shout, all you whose will is justice.

PSALM 33

Rejoice in the Lord, you righteous;
    You who are just, delight in God's praise.
Praise the Lord with a harp;
    Praise God with a ten-stringed lyre.

Sing a new song to God;
  Play well, while you shout for joy.
For the word of the Lord is justice,
  And all God's actions are true.
God loves what is right and just;
  The Lord's constant love fills the world.
By the word of the Lord the skies were made;
  By the breath of God's mouth, all the stars.
God gathered the seas in heaps,
  And piled up stores of deep water.
Let every land be in awe of the Lord;
  Fear God, all you who live on the earth.
For God speaks, and it comes to be;
  God commands, and there it stands.
The Lord destroys the counsel of nations,
  And frustrates the peoples' plans.
The Lord's designs will stand forever;
  God's plans will outlast every age.
Happy the nations whose God is the Lord,
  The people chosen as God's possession.
The Lord gazes down from the skies,
  And sees all of Adam's descendants;
God looks from the throne on high
  At all who live on the earth.
God alone shapes their hearts,
  And evaluates all their deeds.
No king is victorious through great might,
  Nor is a strong man secure in his power;
How vain the swift horse with which to escape:
  No matter how mighty, none save themselves!
Your eye, O Lord, is on those who fear you,
  On those who wait for your mercy.
You will save them from death,
  And keep them alive through famine.
We ourselves wait for you, Lord;
  You are our help and shield.
For in you our hearts find their joy,
  And we trust in your holy name.
May your constant care, Lord, be with us,
  Who patiently wait for you.

PSALM 34

I will bless the Lord at all times;
   God's praise will constantly be in my mouth.
My very being exults in the Lord;
   The poor will hear and rejoice.
Declare the Lord's greatness with me,
   And let us together lift up God's name.
The Lord whom I sought has answered me,
   And saved me from all that frightens me.
Look at the Lord, and be radiant!
   Do not let your face look ashamed.
Poor as I am, I cried out, and God heard;
   The Lord saved me from all that distressed me.
The Lord's messenger camps around us,
   And saves all those who fear God.
Taste and see that the Lord is good;
   Happy are those whose refuge is God.
Stand in awe of the Lord, holy people;
   Those who fear God are never in need.
While even young lions are poor and hungry,
   Those who seek God lack nothing good.
Come, children, listen to me;
   I will teach you the fear of the Lord:
Do you desire long life,
   Yearning for days to enjoy good things?
Then keep your tongue from everything hurtful,
   Your lips from speaking deceit;
Turn from wrong, and do what is right,
   Persistently seeking peace.
God does not countenance those who do wrong,
   But blots out the world's recollection of them.
The eye of the Lord watches over the righteous;
   The ears of the Lord hear their cry for help.
God listens when they cry out,
   And saves them from every distress.
The Lord is close to the brokenhearted,
   And saves the crushed in spirit.
Great distress still comes to the righteous,
   But they are rescued out of it all.

God protects all their bones,
  So that not one bone is broken.
Let evil kill those who wrong others;
  Condemn those who hate good people.
But Lord, redeem the lives of your servants;
  Do not condemn those who seek safety in you.

PSALM 35

Condemn my accusers, Lord;
  Battle my adversaries.
Put on your armor and shield,
  And arise in my defense!
Prepare to hurl your spear,
  And close to meet my pursuers.
Say to me in my weakness,
  "I will be your savior."
Shame those who seek my life;
  Let them be disgraced.
Let those who are trying to wrong me
  Turn back in humiliation,
Like chaff that blows in the wind,
  Driven before the Lord's angel!
Let their roads be dark and slippery,
  While the angel of God pursues them.
Unjustly they set for me traps and snares;
  For no reason they dig pits to kill me.
Let ruin take them by surprise;
  Let their own nets entrap them—
    Let them fall to their destruction.
My inmost self will shout to the Lord,
  And rejoice in God's saving power.
All my bones shall declare:
  "Lord, who could be like you?
You save the weak from those who are stronger,
  The weak and poor from those who rob them."
Vicious perjurors rise to confront me;
  They accuse me of things about which I know nothing.

They repay me with evil when I have been good;
  They are trying to ambush and kill me.
Yet I was in mourning when they were ill,
  I weakened myself with fasting.
My prayers for them were constant,
  As though for a brother or friend.
I acted as though I were mourning my mother;
  I stooped like someone grieving.
Then, when I stumbled, they rejoiced!
  They banded together against me.
They beat me, and I never knew why;
  They tore me to pieces, and would not stop.
They poured out their impious scorn,
  Gnashing their teeth against me.
How long, O Lord, will you stand by?
  Rescue me from their malice;
    Save my poor self from these lions!
In the great congregation I'll thank you;
  Among many peoples, I'll praise you.
Frustrate my enemies' pointless laughter,
  Their hateful, mocking glances.
They never talk of peace;
  Instead, against those who are gentle and patient,
    They hatch their deceitful schemes.
Their mouths gape open against me,
  Saying, "Oh, yes! We know!
    We can see it all!"
Do not be blind and deaf, O Lord!
  Do not be far away, my God!
Wake up! Arise to judge my case;
  My Lord God, vindicate me!
Judge me, Lord God, in your justice;
  Don't let them rejoice over me.
Don't let them say, "This is just what we wanted!"
  Don't let them say, "We ate that one alive!"
Let those who rejoiced at my troubles
  Be utterly shamed and despised.
Let those who boasted against me
  Be clothed in shame and disgrace.
But those who sought justice for me—

May they shout and laugh aloud,
    Never ceasing to say:
"How great you are, O Lord;
    How pleased you are when your servants prosper!"
My tongue, too, will declare your justice,
    And praise you all day long.

PSALM 36

From the depths of my heart, an oracle
    About the revolt of the wicked—
They have no fear of God,
    And do not see why they should!
How admirable they think they are,
    While finding ways to express their hate!
Their mouths speak fraud and betrayal;
    They no longer know how to do good.
They plan treachery even lying in bed!
    They arrive at some no-good course of action,
        Never rejecting that which is wrong.

Your mercy, Lord, is as high as the skies,
    And your faithfulness reaches the clouds.
Your righteousness towers higher than mountains;
    Your justice is deeper than any abyss.
You rescue both people and animals, Lord;
    How precious is your persistent mercy!
Both mortal and immortal beings
    May hide in the shade of your wings;
They are fed from your rich estate,
    And drink from your stream of delights.
From you comes the fountain of life,
    And the light we see is the light that is you.
Extend your mercy to those who know you;
    Be faithful to those whose will is justice.
Do not let the arrogant tread me down;
    Do not let their power drive me from my home.
Look there! The ones who wrong others have fallen!
    They are thrown down, unable to rise!

PSALM 37

Don't be enraged over those who harm others;
   Don't be jealous of unjust people.
They will dry up as quickly as grass;
   Like green plants, they will wither away.
Trust in the Lord, and do what is good;
   Live on the earth, and faithfully tend it.
Take great delight in the Lord,
   Who grants you your deepest desires.
Turn all your plans over to God;
   Have faith, and the Lord will act.
God comes to save you, as sure as the dawn;
   Your vindication will be like the noonday.
Be still before the Lord,
   And tremble before your God;
But don't be enraged by successful schemers,
   By those who carry out evil plots.
Let your anger cease; put your wrath aside.
   Do not, I say, be enraged by the wicked.
For those who harm others will be cut off;
   But the earth be theirs who wait for the Lord.
Soon evil people will cease to exist;
   You will look, but they will not be there.
The earth will belong to lowly people,
   And peace will greatly refresh them.
Wrongdoers plot against the righteous,
   And gnash their teeth against them.
But the Lord laughs at those evil people,
   Knowing their day is coming!
Wrongdoers draw their swords;
   They aim their bows and arrows,
To fell the poor and helpless,
   To slaughter those who act justly.
Their swords will pierce their own hearts;
   Their bows will be cracked and broken.
Better the little wealth of the just
   Than the great and rich displays of the evil!
For the arrows of evil people are broken,
   While it is the Lord who sustains the righteous.

God cares for the blameless as long as they live,
  And their heirs are sustained forever.
In evil times the just know no shame,
  But are fed in the days of famine.
The oppressors, the foes of the Lord,
  Are those who are ruined, and perish.
Like grass that burns in a pasture,
  They will go up in smoke.
The wicked borrow, and never repay,
  While the righteous are generous givers.
Those blessed by God will inherit the earth,
  But the accursed are cut down.
The Lord appoints each person's journey,
  God is pleased to see them progress.
If they fall, they will not be overthrown;
  The hand of the Lord supports them.
Once I was young, and now I am old;
  I never have seen the just abandoned,
    Nor their children begging for food.
Every day they lend generous aid,
  And their children become a blessing.
Turn from evil and do what is good,
  And then you will live forever.
For the Lord is devoted to justice,
  And never abandons the faithful.
The unjust are destroyed forever;
  The oppressor's family is brought to an end.
Those who are just will inherit the earth,
  And live upon it forever.
The righteous talk of wisdom;
  Their tongues discuss true justice.
God's instruction is in their minds;
  Their feet will never stumble.
The wicked lie in wait for the just,
  Seeking to ambush and slay them.
But the Lord will not leave us in their power;
  Nor let them wrongly prevail in court.
Wait for the Lord! Obey God's ways!
  God will raise you to own the world;
    You will see the wicked cut down.

I saw the wicked tyrants
   Flourish like trees in bloom;
I came again, and they were gone;
   I searched, and they were not to be found.
Observe the blameless; look at the upright.
   They all at last find peace.
But rebels are altogether destroyed;
   In the end, oppressors are ruined.
Deliverance comes to the just from the Lord,
   Their fortress in times of distress.
The Lord will rescue and save them;
   Those who seek refuge in God are saved,
     And redeemed from those who oppress them.

PSALM 38

Do not condemn me, Lord, in your anger,
   Nor discipline me in your wrath.
Your arrows have deeply pierced me;
   Your hand is pressing me down.
No healthy spot is left in my flesh,
   Because of your curse on me.
No peace remains in my bones,
   Because of my sin against you.
My guilt is piled up over my head,
   A heavy load, too heavy for me!
My wounds are foul with infection,
   Because I have been so stupid.
I am greatly distressed and humbled;
   I wander dressed in rags all day.
My loins are filled with feverish pain;
   No healthy spot is left in my flesh.
I am so feeble and broken!
   I groan from my pounding heart.
Lord, all my longings are known to you;
   None of my sighs is hidden from you.
My heart is throbbing; my strength has left me.
   Light for my eyes is no longer with me.

My closest friends shun me because of my pain;
  My neighbors keep their distance.
Those who want me dead set snares;
  Those who wish me harm speak threats—
    All day long they mutter their lies.
But I, like someone deaf, do not hear;
  Like a mute, I never open my mouth.
I have become like those who hear nothing,
  Who have no retort in their mouths.
For you, O Lord, I wait in hope;
  You will respond, my Lord and my God.
I am sure my foes will not triumph against me,
  Or get to boast as I stumble and fall.
But I am prepared to be lame,
  And always aware of my pain.
So I declare my guilt,
  And bear the dread of my sin.
How many hate me without any cause!
  I have numerous foes for no reason!
They repay me evil for good;
  They accuse me rather than seek to help me.
Do not abandon me, Lord!
  My God, do not be far from me!
Hurry to be my helper;
  Lord, you are my salvation.

PSALM 39

I promised that I would watch what I did,
  And keep from sin in what I said.
I kept a muzzle over my mouth
  Whenever someone wicked was near.
I kept my thoughts to myself,
  Silent even around good people.
My pain cut me off from others;
  My heart became hot within me.
In my groans, a fire was burning;
  I spoke out with my tongue—

Lord, let me know what my end will be;
  How many days do I have?
    I know how transitory I am!
My span of life is the span of my hand;
  All my days are as nothing to you.
The strength of a person is mere illusion.
  Truly we all are wandering shades.
We work for a heap of illusory wealth—
  Who knows who will gather it in when we die?
But now, Lord, I eagerly wait for you;
  You are my only hope.
Save me from all my rebellious deeds;
  Do not leave me disgraced like a fool!
Silent, I will not open my mouth;
  For you alone must act.
Remove your affliction from me;
  I perish from the blow of your hand.
You punish each one of us for our guilt;
  You melt our wealth away like mist.
    All of us are illusions!
Hear my prayer, O Lord;
  Listen when I cry for help.
    Do not be deaf to my weeping.
I live as a stranger before you,
  Like all my forebears, an alien.
Be gracious to me, and let me find joy,
  Before I depart, and am no more.

PSALM 40

Oh, how I longed for the Lord,
  And God bent down, and heard my cry,
And brought me up from a desolate pit,
  Out of the muddy clay,
And set my feet on a rock,
  Making my steps firm and sure,
And put in my mouth a new song,
  A song of praise for our God.
Many people will see, and be awed,
  And will put their trust in the Lord.

Blessed are those who do so—
   Who put their trust in the Lord—
And do not turn to false gods
   That deceive them and lead them astray.
You have done great things;
   Lord God, you have worked such wonders.
And your intentions for us—
   No one can compare to you!
I could go on talking and talking;
   Your deeds are too many to tell.
You want no sacrificial gifts—
   You carved out my ears, I hear you;
You seek no offerings for sin or praise,
   So I said, "I will simply bring myself."
I desire to do what pleases my God,
   To have your teaching deep within me.
I bring good news to the whole congregation;
   Lord, you know that I am not silent!
I don't hide your justice within my own mind;
   I speak of your true power to save us.
I do not conceal your loyal love
   Or your truth from the great congregation.
Lord, don't withhold your compassion from me;
   May your faithful love always protect me.
For wrongs past counting surround me;
   My sins overtake me and blind me.
They outnumber the hairs on my head,
   And all my courage has left me.
O Lord, be willing to save me;
   Hurry, O Lord, to help me.
Completely shame and humiliate those
   Who seek to take my life.
Let them turn back in disgrace
   For wanting to hurt me.
Let them shudder with shame
   Who laughed aloud at me.
But let all those who seek you
   Be joyful and happy in you.
Let those who love your salvation declare:
   "The Lord is eternally great!"

But I am wretched and poor;
  Consider me, O Lord!
It is you who rescue and aid me;
  My God, do not delay!

PSALM 41

Blessed are those who know they are helpless;
  On the day of disaster, the Lord will save them.
The Lord keeps them alive, and will bless them on earth,
  And will not let their foes prevail over them.
You strengthen them, Lord, on their sickbeds;
  As they rest, you relieve their pain.
I say, "Lord, be gracious to me;
  Heal me, for I have sinned against you."
My foes say horrible things against me;
  They hope I will die, and then be forgotten.
And even if they come to see me,
  Their intent is only to lie;
They come to gather falsehoods,
  To gossip after they leave.
My enemies whisper together about me;
  Most High God, they plan evil against me.
I feel their malicious words pour over me;
  They hope I will never get up from my bed.
Even my closest friend, whom I trusted,
  Who shared my meals, now utterly scorns me.
But you, Lord, be gracious and lift me up,
  And I will take revenge on them.
Then I will know you are pleased with me,
  And will not let my foes rejoice at my death.
As for me, hold me fast in my innocence,
  And let me stand in your presence forever.

[Blessed be the Lord,
  The God of Israel from of old and forever!
    Amen and amen.]

PSALMS 42 and 43

As a deer may pant for streams of water,
  So I pant for you, O God.
I thirst for the living God;
  Where can I go to see God's face?
Day and night my tears are my food,
  As I hear all day long, "Where is your God?"
I pour myself out before God;
  I recall how it used to be—
How I came through the walls, bowing down to God's
    house,
  A great crowd dancing
    And singing God's praise.
How I am melted away,
  So restless within myself!
I wait for God, whom I will praise,
  My God and my true salvation.

I remember you, though I melt away,
  Descending into the nether world,
Where chaotic seas crash to and fro,
  And your towering waves wash over me.
Lord, may you order each day in mercy;
  Each night may I sing a prayer
    To you, the God of my life.
I say to you, my God,
  "Why has my rock forgotten me?
Why do I walk in gloom,
  Hard-pressed by enemies?"
My oppressors' taunts are killing me,
  As they say all day, "Where is your God?"
How I am melted away,
  So restless within myself!
I wait for God, whom I will praise,
  My God and my true salvation.

Bring judgment against this merciless foe!
  Save me from this vicious traitor!
God, my sole refuge, why have you left me?

Why do I walk in gloom,
  Hard-pressed by my enemies?
Send your true light to lead me;
  Bring me home to your holy mountain.
And I will go to God's altar,
  To God my delight and joy;
I will praise you with harps—
  O God, you are my God.
How I am melted away,
  So restless within myself!
I wait for God, whom I will praise,
  My God and my true salvation.

PSALM 44

We have heard, O God, with our own ears,
  Our fathers related to us,
How you did such deeds in their days,
  In days now past, with your own hand.
You dispossessed nations to transplant our ancestors;
  You drove people like sheep, and sent them away.
For not by the sword did we gain this land;
  Our own strong arms did not save us.
It was your right hand and mighty arm;
  The light of your face was their sign of your favor.

You are still my king, my God;
  Command the salvation of Jacob's descendants!
With you, we are rams who smash our oppressors;
  Knowing you, we trample those who confront us.
For I do not trust in my bow;
  It is not my sword that will save me.
It is you who must save me from our oppressors,
  And put to shame those who hate us.
Then we could praise you all day long,
  And celebrate your name forever.

Instead, you reject and abuse us;
  You do not march out with our armies.
You drive us back before our oppressors,
  And those who hate us plunder us.

You feed us to them as though we were sheep,
  And scatter us among the nations.
You sell your people for no price at all;
  You don't even profit from the transaction!
You have disgraced us before our neighbors,
  Those around us mock and deride us.
You have made us a proverb among the nations,
  People recall, and just shake their heads.
My disgrace confronts me all day long,
  And I cover my face in shame,
From the sound of derision and scorn,
  From the sight of the vengeful foe.
All this has happened, yet we don't forget you,
  Nor have we betrayed your covenant.
Our wills have not turned disloyal;
  Our steps have not swerved from your paths.
But you crush us as though we were serpents;
  In the darkest valley you hide us.
If we had forgotten the name of our God,
  And lifted our hands in prayer to a stranger,
Wouldn't you have discovered that,
  Since you know the heart's deepest secrets?
Still, for your sake we are killed all day long;
  We are considered sheep to be slaughtered.
Rouse yourself! Why are you sleeping, Lord?
  Wake up! Can you reject us forever?
Why have you hidden your face?
  Can you forget us, your wretched people?
Our bodies are bowed in the dust;
  Our bellies cling to the ground.
Rise up, and be our helper!
  For your mercy's sake, redeem us!

PSALM 45

My heart responds to a fine occasion;
  I speak to the king my poem.
    My tongue is the pen of a diligent scribe.

Beautiful beyond mere mortals,
   Your lips a fountain of gracious words,
      You are surely blessed by God forever!

Bind your sword upon your thigh—
   Be a splendid, glorious warrior!
Govern and prosper and then ride out
   To establish justice for those who are lowly.
Your right hand shoots with fearful power,
   And peoples fall beneath you—
Your arrows, keen and sharp,
   In the hearts of your foes, O king!
God has enthroned you forevermore;
   And justice will be your royal scepter.
      You love what is just and hate what is wrong;
So God, your God, has anointed you,
   Like no other king, with the oil of joy.
Your robes are cinnamon, aloes, and myrrh;
   In your ivory palace, harps delight you.
And here, with your ladies, a daughter of kings!
   Your chosen consort, with gold from the East.

Hear me, daughter; observe, and listen.
   Forget your people, the house of your father.
The king is your lord, and desires your beauty,
   And you must bow down to him.
Among your gifts is a robe from Tyre;
   The wealthy will flatter and court you.
Here are all a princess's treasures—
   In her garments of gold brocade
      She is led from seamstress to king.
Her maids come after her,
   Brought here to be her companions.
They are brought with laughter and singing;
   They come to the house of the king.

May sons be born to your fathers' line;
   Appoint them as princes throughout the land!
I declare your fame to ages unborn,
   That people may praise you forevermore.

PSALM 46

God is our safety and power;
  We find great help in disaster.
We will not fear if the earth should change,
  If the mountains fall to the depths of the sea,
If the oceans roar and foam,
  If the mountains topple into the valleys.

The Lord of the armies of earth and sky,
  The God of Jacob, our fortress, is with us!

Deep cosmic rivers delight God's city,
  The hallowed home of God Most High.
God is within her; she will not totter.
  God will help her long before dawn.
The nations riot; the kingdoms reel—
  God cries out, and the earth is shaken.

The Lord of the armies of earth and sky,
  The God of Jacob, our fortress, is with us!

Come, see the deeds of the Lord,
  Who sends the earth desolation—
Stopping wars in the world's farthest regions—
  Weapons are shattered, wagons are burned.
"Enough! Admit that I am God,
  High over the nations, high over the world."

The Lord of the armies of earth and sky,
  The God of Jacob, our fortress, is with us!

PSALM 47

Let all nations clap their hands;
  Let all gods shout with laughter.
For the Lord on high is fearful,
  A great king over all the gods,
Making nations submit to us,
  Putting peoples under our feet,
Choosing for us our heritage,
  Jacob's proud land, beloved by God.

God ascends with a shout!
  The Lord, with a trumpet blast!
Sing, you gods, sing out!
  Sing to our king, sing out!
For God rules over all the world;
  Sing a song, all you gods.
God rules over the nations;
  God sits on the holy throne.
The leaders of nations are gathered,
  With us, the people of Abraham's God.
For to God belong the world's rulers;
  God is exalted on high.

PSALM 48

How great is the Lord! How much to be praised,
  In God's own city, God's holy mountain,
    A towering delight for all the world.
Mount Zion, seat of divine authority—
  The great king's capital city.
God is in her fortified towers;
  God is known as Zion's defense.

Now look how the kings are gathered;
  Together they come to attack.
As soon as they see, they are stunned;
  In terror they hurry away.
Here trembling seized them,
  They writhe like women in childbirth.
The ships that sail from Tarsus—
  The east wind shatters them!
Just as we heard, we see for ourselves,
  In the city of the Lord our God;
The Lord of the armies of earth and sky,
  Our God has established this city forever.

Within your temple, O God,
  We reflect on your constant love.
You are praised wherever your story is told,
  As far as the earth's farthest end.
    All that you do brings justice.

Because of your just decisions,
  Mount Zion will sing for joy;
    Judah's towns will shout aloud.
Go all around Mount Zion,
  Counting all her towers.
Think about her wall,
  Examine her fortifications.
Then you can tell generations to come
  That here is God, our God,
    Who leads us forever and ever.

PSALM 49

Listen to this, all peoples;
  Hear, all who live in this world.
Adam's descendants, each human being,
  Both rich and poor alike:
My mouth will say wise things,
  My mind's most discerning thoughts.
My ear is attuned to my proverb;
  With a harp, I reveal my riddle.
Why should I be afraid in bad times,
  Though surrounded by cheaters who trick me?
Those people who trust in their riches,
  And boast of abundant wealth!
Alas, they can never ransom themselves;
  They will find that God is not to be bribed.
They cannot afford the price of a life!
  They come to their everlasting end.
Yet they have no fear of the grave,
  As though they would live forever!
Can't they see? Even wise people die,
  And the shameless and stupid utterly perish,
    And leave all their wealth to others.
The grave is their home forever,
  Their dwelling through all time to come—
    Though doubtless their heirs remember them fondly!
How splendid their tombs, but how soundly they sleep!
  They have become as dumb as cattle.

This is the road the complacent will follow;
  The fate of those who indulge their fancies.
Like sheep they are sent to Sheol;
  Death will be their shepherd,
    And they will justly go down to the grave.
Their bodies will waste away;
  The world of the dead will be their mansion.
"But surely," they say, "God will redeem me!
  God will take me away from death's power!"

Do not be afraid when someone grows rich,
  When their family's wealth increases.
When they die, they can't take it with them;
  Their wealth does not follow them down.
Just because someone seems blessed while they live—
  People praise you when things go well!—
    They still must go with their ancestors.
How splendid their tombs, but how soundly they sleep!
  They have become as dumb as cattle.

PSALM 50

God the Lord spoke out to the world,
  From the rising of the sun to its setting.
God's perfect beauty shines forth from Zion;
  Our God will come and not be silent.
Preceded by devouring flames,
  Surrounded by a mighty tempest,
Addressing the earth and skies,
  God tells them, "Judge my people!
Gather to me my devoted ones,
  Who made a covenant at my altar."
And the skies declare God's verdict,
  For it is God who is judge.

"Listen, my people, and I will speak;
  Israel, I will counsel you.
    I am God, your God.
Not for your sacrifice do I reprove you;
  Your offerings are always before me.

But I will not accept a bull from your herd,
    Nor take a goat from your flock.
For every forest creature is mine,
    And the animals prowling a thousand hills;
I know every bird that flies,
    And all that moves in the fields is with me.
If I were hungry, would I tell you?
    For everything in the world is mine.
Would I eat the flesh of bulls,
    Or drink the blood of goats?
Sacrifice by praising your God,
    Fulfilling your vows to me on high!
And call to me in the day of distress;
    I will save you, and you will glorify me.
Why do you recite my decrees,
    Your mouths declaring my covenant?
Yet you hate to be taught;
    You toss my words behind you.
If you see a thief, you run and help;
    You share in the acts of adulterers.
Your mouth is quick to speak evil;
    You yoke your tongue to deceit.
You turn to speak against your brother;
    You slander your own mother's son.
This you did, and I was silent,
    So you supposed I was just like you!
        Now, to your face, I confront and accuse you.
You, who forget your God, pay attention,
    Lest I tear you to pieces past saving.
Offer your praise, and give me honor.
    With determination, follow the way;
        I will reveal my divine salvation."

PSALM 51

God, in your mercy be gracious to me;
    In your great compassion erase my rebellion.
Cleanse me from guilt, again and again,
    And purify me from my sin.

For too well do I know my rebellion,
    I am always aware of my sin;
Against you alone have I sinned,
    I have done what you despise.
So you are right in your decree;
    So you are blameless in judgment.
Perverse I have been since I was conceived,
    A sinner since my mother bore me.
Truth, not learning, is what you desire,
    Wisdom, not craft, is what you teach me.
Make me cleaner than fresh-flowing water;
    Wash me and I will be whiter than snow.
Invite me to joyous delight,
    Let the bones you have broken rejoice.
Hide your face from my sin,
    And wipe away all my guilt.
Create a pure heart for me, O God;
    Renew within me a steady spirit.
Do not throw me out of your presence;
    Nor take your holy spirit from me.
Bring back to me your joyous salvation,
    Let your spirit freely support me;
Let me teach your ways to rebels,
    Let sinners return to you.
Save me, O God, from deadly guilt;
    My tongue will shout out your justice.
Lord, may you open my lips,
    And my mouth will declare your praise.
I would sacrifice if you wanted;
    You are not pleased by burnt offerings.
God, my gift is a broken will;
    You do not scorn a submissive heart.
[Be good and gracious to Zion;
    Rebuild Jerusalem's walls.
Then receive sacrifice rightly offered;
    Then let bulls be burned on your altar.]

PSALM 52

How the hero boasts in evil,
    Affronting God all day long!
You plan my ruin, working deceit;
    You sharpen your tongue like a knife.
You love evil more than good;
    You'd rather lie than speak the truth.
You love all those who speak to confuse—
    You with your lying tongue!
God will demolish you forever,
    Tearing you right out of your home,
        Uprooting you from the land of the living.

The righteous will see, and fear—
    And then they will laugh at you!
"What a hero you are, to set God aside,
    Rather than let God defend you!
You trusted in all that wealth of yours,
    And defended yourself with your greedy threats!"
But I will be like a flourishing olive tree,
    Planted within the house of God.
I trust in God's devoted love,
    That lasts forever and ever.
I will praise you, eternal God,
    For all that you have done.
I eagerly wait to know you,
    Your goodness to your devoted people.

PSALM 53

Fools convince themselves
    That there is no God.
Their injustice corrupts and destroys;
    Not one does what is good.
The Lord looks down from the sky,
    At all the descendants of Adam.
To see if anyone is wise,
    If anyone seeks for God.

But everyone is disloyal,
  Corrupted altogether;
Not one does what is good,
  Not a single one!

Don't you know, you who do wrong—
  You who devour my people for food—
    Won't they cry to the Lord?
They were terribly afraid,
  Though there was no reason to fear,
For God scatters the bones of your army.
  Be humbled, rejected of God!

Who will bring from the Mount of Zion
  Salvation for Israel?
When the Lord brings back the exiles,
  God's people, Jacob, will celebrate;
    Israel will shout for joy.

PSALM 54

Save me, O God, by your power;
  By your strength bring me justice.
Listen, O God, to my prayer,
  And hear the words of my mouth.
For insolent people rise against me,
  And tyrants are seeking to kill me—
    They seem to care nothing for God.

God in truth is my helper,
  My Lord, who sustains my life.
Let my foes' evil plots turn against them;
  Silence them, Lord, in your faithfulness.
My gifts to you are freely given;
  I praise your righteous power.
For you save me from every distress,
  And I see my enemies' downfall.

PSALM 55

Hear my prayer, O God;
  Do not withdraw from my plea for mercy.
Be attentive to me and answer me,
  My anxious fear overpowers me.
My enemies' voices utterly drain me;
  I cannot face their malicious harassment.
They heap accusations upon me;
  They bring charges against me in anger.
My heart is writhing within me;
  The horrors of death have fallen upon me.
Terror and trembling enter me;
  My whole body is shaking.

I ask, "Who will give me the wings of a dove?
  I will fly away, to live in the wild!
I really would flee, and be homeless,
  And spend my nights in the desert.
I would hurry to find a safe place,
  Away from this storm of slander."
Swallow them up, O Lord;
  Cut their tongues in two!
For I have seen the violence,
  The feuds here in the city.
Day and night they surround this place,
  Surmounting all the walls.
Guilt and disaster live here;
  Here there are only ruins.
Oppression and cruel fraud
  Are never far from our streets.

If it were only foes who reproached me,
  Then I could surely bear it.
If only my enemies boasted against me,
  I would stay hidden from them.
But you, my partner and peer,
  My trusted and well-known friend—
Together we would have sweet conversation,
  Within the house of God!

We used to be occupied in counsel—
   Now let death overtake them!
Let them go down alive to Sheol;
   They store up evil within themselves.
But I will call to God;
   The Lord will rescue me.
At evening, at dawn, at noon,
   I will moan and complain,
And God will hear my voice,
   And pay to ransom my life.
God will be close to me,
   Because there are many against me.
God will hear me and answer,
   And stay with me forever;
In God, whom they refuse to worship,
   Is no inconstancy!
But they reach out against their allies,
   They violate every trust.
Their speech is as smooth as cream,
   But what they intend is war;
Their words are soothing as oil,
   But they have drawn their swords.
Throw your burden upon the Lord,
   Who will surely hold you up.
Not for long will you, O God,
   Allow the just to stumble!
But you, O God, bring down
   The treacherous, violent people.
They descend to the depths of the grave
   Before half their days are over!
      And I will trust in you.

PSALM 56

God, be gracious to me,
   For someone is hounding me all day long;
      They close in to torment me.
My oppressors hound me all day long;
   So many are closing in on me.

Exalted God, when I am afraid,
  I put my faith in you;
    God, I praise you aloud:
"In God I trust; I have no fear.
  What can flesh do to me?"
All day long they find fault with my words;
  All their intentions are hostile to me.
They hide to attack and harm me;
  They watch my tracks in order to kill me.
Save me from them, because they are guilty;
  Throw down these people in anger, O God.
You yourself can write my complaint;
  Record my tears in your scroll—
    Do you not keep a ledger?
Then my foes will turn back,
  On that day when I cry out;
    Then I will know that I have a God!
God, I praise you aloud;
  Lord, I praise you aloud:
"In God I trust; I have no fear—
  What can mere mortals do to me?"
I owe you, O God, what I promised;
  I will repay you with praise.
For you delivered me from death—
  Did you not keep my foot from stumbling?
And so I walk in the presence of God,
  In the light, among the living.

PSALM 57

Be gracious, God; be gracious to me,
  For I seek refuge in you.
In the shade of your wings, I seek refuge,
  Until the threat has gone by.
I will cry out to God Most High,
  To God, who is my avenger.
God sends from the sky and saves me;
  God reviles the people who hound me.

God sends out faithful love;
  God is the one who saves me.
I lie down to sleep in the midst of lions—
  Those who swallow up human beings—
Their teeth are spears and arrows,
  Their tongues a sharpened sword.
Arise beyond the sky, O God;
  Reveal your glory above all the world!
They have set a net for my feet,
  Arranged a noose for my neck;
They dig a pit in front of me—
  They themselves fall into it!
Let my mind be resolute, God,
  Let my mind be resolute.
Let me sing and make music;
  Let my strength awaken.
Let my harp and lyre awaken,
  I will awaken the morning light!
I praise you, Lord, among the nations;
  I sing to you among the peoples.
For great beyond the sky is your love;
  Your faithfulness is above the clouds.
Arise beyond the sky, O God;
  Reveal your glory above all the world!

PSALM 58

False gods, are you really speaking the truth,
  Or fairly judging the human race?
In fact, you do evil upon the earth;
  You make your way with violent hands.

The wicked, wayward from birth, are offensive,
  Speaking their lies from the day they are born.
Their poison is like the poison of serpents;
  Like a cobra gone deaf, they close their ears,
Refusing to hear the sound of the charmer,
  The player who conjures with expert spells.
O God, pull out the fangs from their mouths;
  Shatter the jaws of these lions, O Lord!

As foul as the urine that flows from them,
  They attack in a mindless mob.
Like snails, they dissolve into slime as they move;
  Like stillborn children, they never see sunlight.
Like a thornbush, they stab without ever thinking;
  Their hair bristles, like angry beasts.

The just will rejoice when they see vindication,
  And bathe their feet in the blood of the wicked.
And people will say, "The just are rewarded;
  There are indeed gods who judge the world."

PSALM 59

Save me, my God, from my enemies;
  Shield me from those who rise against me.
Rescue me from those who do wrong;
  Save me from murderous people.
They are already hiding in ambush to kill me;
  They attack me with haughty assurance.
I have never wronged or offended them, Lord;
  They hurry to shoot me although I am innocent.
Wake up when I call you, and look!
    You are the God of Israel,
      The Lord of the armies of earth and sky!
Arise to give all the nations their due;
  Show no mercy to unjust traitors.
At dusk they gather, yelping like dogs,
  And prowl around the city;
Out of their lips and mouths
    They pour their sword-sharp howls—
      And who wants to listen to them?
But you, O Lord, can laugh at them;
  You can ridicule all the nations.
I will leave it to you to deal with their power,
  For you, O God, are my fortress.
May the God to whom I am faithful be near me;
  May God let me look on my foes with disdain.
Do not kill them, lest my people forget;

But shake them with all your might,
    And bring them down, our ruler, our sovereign!
For the words of their lips, their sinful speech,
   Let their own arrogance trap them.
Let them talk of how they are cursed and ill.
   Destroy them in anger; destroy them completely.
They will know that God rules among Jacob's descendants;
   And to the earth's farthest end.
At dusk they gather, yelping like dogs,
   And prowl around the city.
They roam in search of food;
   Finding nothing to eat, they lie down to sleep.
And I will sing of your power,
   And praise your faithfulness every morning.
For you are a fortress for me;
   A place of refuge, when times are hard.
You are my power; I sing to you,
   For you, O God, are my fortress,
     The God to whom I am faithful.

PSALM 60

God, you abandoned us and broke us;
   In anger you have betrayed us.
You destroyed the land; you split it open;
   Heal these rifts; the land is reeling!
You are making us see hard times;
   You make us drink wine that leaves us dazed.
For those who fear you, set up a banner
   Around which to rally against the archers.
Thus will you save your beloved people;
   Your right hand will come down to save us.
God speaks from the sanctuary:
   "I proudly apportion Shechem;
     I measure the valley of Succoth.
Gilead and Manasseh are mine;
   Ephraim crowns my head;
     Judah becomes my royal scepter.
Moab is my basin for washing;

Edom the mat where I toss my shoes.
  I triumph over the Philistines!"
Who will give us the fortified city?
  Who will bring us the throne of Edom?
God, have you not abandoned us?
  You don't go out with our armies!
Give us deliverance from our foes—
  For human aid is useless.
With God we will do a mighty deed;
  God will trample down our oppressors!

PSALM 61

Hear, O God, my cry for help;
  Give my prayer your attention.
In my weakness, I call to you,
  From the farthest edge of the world;
    Lift me high on a rock, and guide me.
For you are a place of refuge for me,
  A tower of strength confronting my foes.
I will always live as a guest in your tent,
  And be safe, concealed by your wings.
For you, O God, have heard my vows;
  You gave me a place among those who fear you.
Add more days to the life of the king;
  Give him years that go on and on.
Appoint as his guardians Truth and Faith,
  As he sits forever enthroned before God.
So I will always sing your name,
  Fulfilling my vows, day after day.

PSALM 62

Only in God can I be serene;
  From God will come my salvation.
Only God is my saving rock;
  My fortress—I will not stumble.

How long will you attack others—
   Murderers, all of you—
As though you were merely tearing down fences,
   Or pushing over an old stone wall?
You scheme to drag people down,
   And you delight in deception;
Out loud you say, "We bless you!"
   But silently you are cursing.

Only in God can I be serene,
   In God alone is my hope.
Only God is my saving rock;
   My fortress—I will not stumble.

My salvation and glory depend upon God,
   My mighty rock, my place of refuge.
All people are just a passing breath;
   The human race is a lie.
If they were weighed in a balance,
   They would be lighter than air.
Put no trust in the wealth you have stolen;
   Do not believe that force will succeed.
Once God has spoken, twice have I heard,
   That power belongs to God,
That you, O Lord, are constant love.
   You repay us each in accord with our deeds.

PSALM 63

O God, my God, I am eager to find you;
   My heart is thirsty for you.
In my weakness I yearn for you,
   As though in a dry and weary land.
I look in your holy place for you,
   To see your strength and glory.
Because your grace is better than life,
   My lips will praise you.
As long as I live, I will bless you;
   I lift up my hands in your name.
I am filled as though with the finest foods,
   And with joyful lips I praise you.

In my bed, remembering you,
  I ponder you in the darkness.
It is you who come to my aid;
  In the shade of your wings I shout for joy.
My inmost self pursues you,
  Your right hand holds me fast.
Some people are trying to trap me,
  But they will be sent to the grave;
The sword will spill their blood,
  And they will be jackals' food.
And our king will rejoice in God;
  His faithful subjects will triumph,
And God will shut the mouths
  Of those who go on telling lies.

PSALM 64

God, listen when I complain;
  And save my life from the fearsome foe.
Hide me from evil peoples' plots,
  And from oppressors' conspiracies.
They sharpen their tongues like swords;
  They aim bitter words like arrows.
From ambush, they shoot the innocent;
  Their attack is sudden and fearless!
They arm themselves with cruel words;
  They discuss how they can conceal their snares.
They say, "Who will notice them?
  We have thought it through: our schemes are perfect."
Oh, the soul and the mind are profound!
  But God will shoot an arrow at them.
Suddenly they will be the wounded,
  And their own tongues will trip them up.
All who see will be deeply shaken,
  Everyone will be terrified.
They will discuss what God has done,
  And come to understand it.
Let the righteous rejoice and seek refuge in God;
  Let all those committed to justice, sing praise.

PSALM 65

Truly, Lord, our praise is for you;
  You are God in Zion.
Our vow to you will be fulfilled;
  Listen to our prayer!
All people must come to you,
  To confess their sin;
Our sins are too much for us;
  May you forgive them!
What a joy when you choose to be near,
  When one can live in your courts!
Let blessing fill your house,
  Let your temple be holy.
You confront us with fearful justice,
  You, our saving God.
You can be trusted in earth's far regions
  And on the most distant sea.
In your strength you establish mountains;
  They are held tight by your power.
You quiet the roaring seas,
  The tumult of waves and the uproar of nations.
Those who live far away fear your omens;
  At the gateways of day and night they cry out.

It is you who make the soil productive;
  Make it abundantly rich!
Fill the sky-channels with water;
  Bring up the planted grain.
Drench the furrows, level the ridges;
  Dissolve them with gentle showers.
Bless the tiny shoots;
  Crown the furrows with your great bounty.
Let oil flow in the planted rows;
  Let oil from olives flow in the fields.
Clothe the hills with rejoicing.
  Robe the mountains in flocks of sheep,
Mantle the valleys with grain.
  All nature, shout and sing for joy!

PSALM 66

Let all the world shout to God;
  Sing God's glorious name,
    And offer glorious praise.
Say to God, "Your work is so awesome!
  You are so strong, your foes cringe before you."
To you the whole world bows down;
  Singing to you, singing your fame:
"Come and see what God has done—
  No mortal could do such a fearful deed—
God changed the sea to dry land,
  The people passed through the flood on foot.
    Now let us rejoice in God!"
God rules from an everlasting fortress,
  Watching attentively over the nations
    Lest rebels arise from among them.
Bless our God, you nations;
  Let your voice be heard in praise!
It is God who made us come alive,
  And keeps our feet from stumbling.
Yet you have tested us, God;
  You refined us as though refining silver.
You brought us into the desert;
  You afflicted our bodies with hardship,
    And burdened our heads with pain.
But when we had gone through water and fire,
  We were led to this land of plenty.
I will go to your house with gifts,
  To fulfill what I promised to you,
When I opened my lips to speak
  And I spoke out loud in distress.
I offer living sacrifices—
  The ram I offer with incense,
    The goats as well as the bull.
Come, you worshippers, hear me relate
  What God has done for me.
My mouth called out to God,
  And my cry was upon my tongue;

If I had seen guilt in my heart,
  My Lord would not have listened;
Nevertheless, God listened,
  And heard the sound of my prayer.
I will bless you, O God;
  You did not reject my prayer,
    Nor deny your grace to me.

PSALM 67

Knowing your way on the earth,
  Your saving work in all countries,
The peoples will praise you, God;
  The peoples all will praise you.
Nations will shout and rejoice,
  For you rule the peoples fairly,
    And guide the nations on earth.

The peoples will praise you, God;
  The peoples all will praise you.
Let the earth yield her produce;
  Let God, our God, now bless us.
Bless us; you are our God!
  Then we will worship you
    In all the world's farthest regions.

PSALM 68

Rise up, O God! Let your foes be scattered!
  Let those who hate you flee from your presence!
Let them be blown away like smoke;
  Melted like wax that is close to the fire,
    Let the guilty perish before God's face!
Then the just will be glad;
  They will delight in God's presence,
    They will rejoice and be happy.
Sing to the Lord! Sing out God's name!

Make way for the One who rides the clouds.
Exult in the God whose name is the Lord.
Father of orphans, defender of widows,
God is in the holy temple.
God, who gives the lonely a home,
Who brings the prisoners out with singing;
But stubborn rebels must camp in the desert!
God, when you came to meet your people,
When you strode out from the wilderness—
The land trembled, the sky was shaken,
Before the Lord, who comes from Sinai,
Before the Lord, who is Israel's God.
God, you send the generous showers.
You have secured your triumphant heritage.
Here your domain will be settled;
God, you provide for the poor in your goodness.
The Lord will declare a message,
Good news to a mighty army!
Kings with their forces run to hide;
And the victors' daughters divide the spoil—
Unlike you who hid in the gulleys!
Wings of a dove modeled in silver,
With feathers of finest gold,
Where the God of the mountain scattered kings,
Where snow fell down on the Mountain of Darkness.
O mighty mountain, Mount Bashan,
High-arched mountain, Mount Bashan,
Why view with envy, high-arched mountain,
The precious mountain of God's own dwelling,
The place where the Lord will dwell forever?
God's chariots numbered twice ten thousand,
Along with thousands of archers;
The Lord is on Sinai in holiness.
You, O God, went up to the height;
You took prisoners of war.
You took ransoms from them, Lord God,
And settled the proud in the place you chose.
Blessed be the Lord, day after day,
Our saving God who gives all that we ask.

This is our God—the God of salvation;
　The Lord, who was our escape from death.
How God smote the heads of the enemy,
　The skulls of those who acted wrongly!
The Lord says, "I came from high Bashan,
　I came from the depths of the sea,
That you might wash your feet in blood,
　And apportion your foes among your dogs."
They see you marching forth, O Lord;
　My God is marching forth,
　　My king from the holy place.
Singers in front, harpists behind,
　In the middle, the drum-playing marchers.
In great assemblies, bless the Lord—
　Your Lord, you assemblies of Israel!
See little Benjamin leading them;
　Then princes of Judah in purple robes,
　　Zebulun's princes, Naphtali's princes.
Send your strength, O God;
　Strengthen what you have done for us.
Your temple is in Jerusalem;
　Kings will bring gifts to you.
Rebuke the beast from the banks of the Nile,
　The herd of bulls and calves—
Eager for wealth, they trample nations,
　Delighting in conflict, scattering peoples.
So bring from Egypt purple cloth;
　Cush, stretch out your hands in prayer.
Kingdoms of earth, sing praise;
　Sing, you gods, to the Lord,
To the rider of the primeval skies,
　Who thunders with a mighty voice!
Give the glory to God,
　Who is high over Israel,
　　Whose power transcends the heavens.
Fearful is God in the holy temple;
　Bless the Lord our God!
Truly the God of Israel
　Will give to the people strength and power.

PSALM 69

Deliver me, O God,
  For the water is up to my neck!
I am sinking into deep mud,
  And have no place to stand.
I have come into deep rivers,
  And the torrent will sweep me away.
I am exhausted from crying out;
  My throat is hoarse, my eyes grow bleary,
    Waiting for you, my God.
Those who hate me for nothing
  Outnumber the hairs on my head.
I have more lying enemies than bones;
  They make me return things I never stole.
God, you know how foolish I am,
  And my guilty deeds are not hidden from you.
Do not let me shame those who wait for you—
  Lord God of the armies of earth and sky;
Let me not bring disgrace to those who seek you—
  You are the God of Israel.
For your sake I endure reproach;
  I cover my face in shame,
Estranged from my brothers and sisters—
  To my own mother's children, an alien!
My zeal for your house consumes me,
  And those who scorn you, scorn me.
I weep, and I eat no food;
  This is such a disgrace for me!
I put on my roughest clothes;
  I am a proverb for those around me—
The topic of gossip in city squares,
  The subject of drunkards' songs.
But still I pray to you, O Lord,
  For a time when you will be kind.
Respond to me, God, in your great love,
  In the constancy of your saving will.
Save me from this mud; don't let me sink.
  Protect me from this torrent of hatred.

Don't let this river sweep me away;
　Don't let these depths swallow me up.
　　Don't let the pit close its mouth around me.

Respond to me, Lord, with your constant goodness;
　Turn to me in your great compassion.
Do not hide your face from me, your servant—
　I am so hard-pressed; hurry, and answer.
Come close to me, and redeem my life;
　Ransom me from my enemies' power.
You yourself know my disgrace,
　The shame and abuse that are mine;
　　Right before you are all my foes.
Awful disgrace has broken my heart;
　I looked for comfort, and there was none;
　　For reassurance, and could not find it.
Instead of food, they gave me poison;
　To quench my thirst they let me drink vinegar.
Let their banquets be traps for them;
　Let their friendly feasts be snares!
Darken their eyes, that they may not see;
　Let their legs be completely unstable.
Pour your anger upon them;
　Let your fiery wrath overtake them.
Let their camp be deserted;
　Let no one inhabit their tents.
They harass people you have already punished,
　Detailing the pain that you have inflicted.
Give them the punishment they deserve;
　Let them not come to be pardoned by you.
Erase their names from the book of the living;
　Do not enroll them among the just.
But I am wounded and helpless;
　O God, let your saving power defend me.
I will praise God's greatness with singing;
　I will offer my hearty thanksgiving,
More pleasing to God than sacrifice,
　Than the offering of four-footed creatures.
The oppressed will see, and rejoice;
　Those who seek God will regain their strength.

For the Lord does hear the poor,
   And does not despise the people in prison.
Skies and earth will praise our God,
   Seas, and all their teeming creatures.
For God will deliver Mount Zion,
   And rebuild the cities of Judah.
Those who truly love God will live here;
   This place will belong to their children.
     They will possess and inhabit this place.

PSALM 70

O God, if you will save me,
   Hurry, O Lord, to help me.
Completely shame and humiliate those
   Who seek to take my life.
Let them turn back in disgrace,
   For wanting to hurt me.
Let them withdraw in shame
   Who laughed aloud at me.
But let all those who seek you,
   Be joyful and happy in you.
Let those who love your salvation declare,
   "The Lord is eternally great!"
But I am wretched and poor;
   Hurry to me, O God!
It is you who rescue and aid me;
   O Lord, do not delay!

PSALM 71

In you, Lord, I seek refuge;
   Eternal One, do not shame me.
In your justice deliver and rescue me;
   Listen to me, and help me.
Be my house on a rock;
   You have promised always to save me,
     For you are my rock and my stronghold.

Save me from the oppressor's grasp,
  From the grip of an evil robber.
For you are my hope, O Lord,
  The God I have trusted since childhood.
Since I was born, I have leaned on you;
  Since my life began, you have strengthened me.
I have become a sign for many;
  You are my strong refuge.
My mouth is full of your praise
  And your splendor, all day long.
Do not toss me aside in my old age;
  When my strength fails, do not abandon me.
For my enemies speak out against me;
  They plot and watch for a chance to kill me,
Saying, "There is one whom God has abandoned,
  Whom we can pursue and seize,
    For whom there is no escape."

God, do not be far from me;
  My God, hurry to help me.
Let those who wish me to die
  Be consumed by humiliation.
Let those who seek to harm me
  Be seized by disgrace and shame.
My mouth will declare your justice
  And your saving power, all day long,
    Though they are greater than I can tell.

I come and go in the strength of my Lord;
  I proclaim that justice is yours alone.
God, you have taught me since childhood;
  Since then I have told of your wonders.
Even in my advanced old age,
  God, do not abandon me.
Let me talk of your strength to the next generation;
  Your mighty justice, that reaches the sky.
You have done great things;
  O God, who is like you?
You show us many terrible hardships,
  Only to turn and restore our lives;
    From the depths of the earth you raise us up.

You multiply my resources;
　　You surround me and comfort me.
So I will thank you, singing aloud,
　　For your faithfulness, my God;
With a harp, I will sing to you,
　　Israel's Holy One.
Not only my lips will sing out to you,
　　But my very soul, that you redeemed;
All day my tongue will proclaim your justice,
　　For those who sought to harm me
　　　　Are so disgraced and shamed!

PSALM 72

O God, let the king be righteous;
　　Let the heir to the throne be just.
Let him plead the cause of your people;
　　Let the poor obtain true justice.
Let the mountains declare, "God's people are innocent!"
　　And the hills, "We are setting them free!"
May he help the oppressed find justice,
　　Save the poor, and crush the exploiter.
Let him outlive the sun and the moon,
　　Through all generations to come.
Let him fall like rain on the grass,
　　Like showers sprinkling the earth.
Throughout his reign let justice bloom
　　In plenty and peace, while the moon endures.
Let him be king from sea to sea,
　　From the river Euphrates to earth's farthest end.
Let his enemies kneel before him;
　　Let his foes all lick the dust.
Let kings to the north and west bring tribute;
　　Let kings to the south and east bring gifts.
Let all the kings bow before him;
　　Let all the nations serve him.
For he saves the poor when they cry for help,
　　The oppressed when no one will aid them.

He cares for the helpless poor,
   And gives life to all the oppressed,
Redeeming them from cruel extortion
   Because he values their lives.
He devotes his life to them,
   And gives them Arabia's wealth.
He constantly prays for their welfare,
   And blesses them every day.
Let grain abound in the land,
   Let it wave on the mountaintops!
Let the harvest bloom as in Lebanon,
   In the cities as much as the fields!
Let his name live forever,
   Let his descendants outshine the sun.
Let all nations seek his blessing,
   And find themselves blessed in him.

[Blessed be the Lord, Israel's God,
   Who alone does marvelous things;
Blessed be God's eternal name,
   And let God's glory fill the world.
     Amen and amen.
The end of the prayers of David, Jesse's son.]

PSALM 73

How good God is to the upright,
   To those whose purpose is pure!
But I nearly lost my footing;
   My feet were almost pulled from beneath me.
For I was jealous of foolish people—
   I saw how oppressors prospered.
They seemed not to suffer at all;
   Instead, their bodies grew fat.
They took no part in mortal struggles;
   They seemed to be human, yet nothing hurt them!
So their necklace was arrogance;
   They dressed themselves in cruelty.
Their eyes bulged out from fat;
   They ignored what their hearts were saying.

They scornfully spoke of evil;
   They loftily spoke of extortion.
They spoke as though they were gods in the sky;
   Their tongues were strutting across the land.
So they completely gorged themselves;
   They drank up the sea in their greed.
They thought, "How could God ever know?
   Is God on high aware at all?"
That is how the oppressors are—
   Always at ease, increasing their wealth.
All in vain have I kept my heart pure,
   And washed my hands in innocence!
For I am injured all day long,
   From early morning they criticize me.

But when I decide to talk like this,
   I mislead the assembly of your own children.
Yet, if I try to understand it
   The effort is more than my mind can bear,
Until I go to God's sanctuary,
   And see what their end will be.
You really have put them in slippery places!
   You bring them down through their own self-deceptions.
How suddenly they will be horribly ruined,
   Completely swept away in terror!
Like a dream that is gone when the dreamer awakes,
   Their ghosts will be unworthy of notice.
Whenever my mind is bitter,
   Or I feel myself cut to the heart,
Then I am foolish, without understanding,
   As dumb as a cow in relation to you.
For I am always with you:
   You hold my hand in yours.
You guide me with your own counsel;
   You lead me toward your glory.
Whom do I have in the sky except you?
   Other than you I have no one on earth.
My body and mind will come to an end;
   Eternal God, you are all I have!
But those who wander away from you—
   You silence all who are faithless to you.

But for me, the nearness of God is best;
   Lord God, I have made you my refuge,
     That I may speak of all your deeds.

PSALM 74

Why, O God, reject us forever,
   Seething against the sheep of your pasture?
Remember your people you long ago ransomed;
   You redeemed this tribe to be your own,
     To live with you on Mount Zion.
Lift up your people from total ruin;
   The foe has destroyed your entire temple.
In your place of worship, your enemies roared,
   And set up their flags as signs of their power.
Like those who climb the high trees,
   And hack the branches with axes,
They utterly leveled the lofty gates;
   They cut them down with their hatchets and crowbars.
Your sanctuary they set ablaze;
   They completely defiled the place where you lived.
They thought, "Let us burn them, root and branch,
   Every place in the land where God can be worshipped."
We cannot see what these things can mean;
   We no longer have a prophet,
     And none of us know how long this will last.
God, how long will oppressors taunt us?
   Will enemies mock your name forever?
Why do you hold back your power,
   Just folding your arms across your chest?
From birth you have been my sovereign God,
   Working salvation here in this world.
You shake sea monsters with your strength,
   And break the dragon's heads in the water.
You crush Leviathan's head,
   And feed the corpse to sharks in the sea.
You open up springs and streams,
   Or dry up the flowing rivers.

Both day and night belong to you;
    You set the bright sun in place.
You establish all earth's boundaries;
    You form the summer and winter.
Recall, then, Lord, how the enemy scorns you,
    How a stupid people mocks your name.
Don't give your frail dove to the beasts—
    Don't forget the life of the poor forever.
Be true to your covenant! We fulfill it,
    While violence haunts our darkened land.
Do not let the humble remain disgraced;
    Let lowly and poor people praise your name.
Get up, O God! Argue your case!
    Remember how fools reproached you all day!
Do not forget the cry of your foes,
    In constant uproar, rebelling against you.

PSALM 75

We praise you, O God; we praise you.
    We call to you by name,
        Declaring your wonderful deeds—
It is you who said, "I summon the council;
    I will judge the righteous.
You, the world's disheartened inhabitants—
    I have established the world's foundations!
I said to the fools, 'Do not be deluded!'
    I told the oppressors, 'Do not be proud!'"
Do not be proud of your high position,
    You who speak with stiff-necked arrogance!
For not by Dawn or Dusk,
    Not by the desert hills—
By God will you be judged,
    The God who lifts one and casts down another.
The cup is in the hand of the Lord,
    Full of wine that is mixed with fire!
God pours it out; it drains to the dregs—
    And all the world's oppressors must drink it!

And I will speak to God everlasting,
   And sing to the God of Jacob.
God will cut off the horns of the wicked,
   And exalt the horns of the just.

PSALM 76

May God be revealed in Judah,
   God's name be great in Israel!
May the tent of God be in Salem,
   The dwelling of God in Zion.
There God shattered the deadly bow,
   Shield and sword, and war itself.

You are fearful,
   More mighty than beasts of prey.
The strong and courageous are plundered;
   They found their eternal rest.
Mighty heroes failed
   To find their former power.
Because of your threats, O God of Jacob,
   The chariot-riders slumbered.
You indeed are fearful!
   Who can stand before you,
     In the face of your mighty wrath?
You make judgment sound from the skies;
   The earth fears, and finds peace,
When God arises in justice,
   To save all the afflicted on earth.
You are crowned with anger against our race;
   Your sash is your destroying rage.

Fulfill your vows to the Lord your God;
   Let God be surrounded by those who bring tribute,
     Who bring their gifts to the fearful God—
The God who humbles the spirit of princes,
   The God who is feared by the kings of this world.

PSALM 77

I cried aloud to God;
  I cried to God, who heard me.
In a day of distress I sought my Lord—
  My lifted hands implored all night;
    My inmost self would not be consoled.
Remembering God, I am restless;
  I ponder God, and my spirit is faint.
I make my eyes stay open;
  Speechless, I pace the floor.
I think of historic days,
  Remembering years long past.
I meditate deeply all night;
  I ponder my spirit's hidden ways.
Will the Lord reject us forever,
  And never befriend us again?
God, will you always hold back your grace?
  Age after age, will you speak no more?
God, have you forgotten pity,
  Or shut off compassion with anger?
I said, "Let me compose a song,
  Of the High God's years of power—
Recalling the deeds of the Lord,
  Recalling your ancient wonders."
I meditate on all your works;
  I ponder all your actions.
God, you act in holy ways;
  Who is a mighty god like God?
You are God, doing wonderful things,
  Revealing your power to nations.
With your arm you redeemed your people,
  The offspring of Jacob and Joseph.
The waters saw you, O God;
  The waters saw you and writhed in terror.
    The deeps were shaking with fear.
Water streamed from the clouds;
  The storm clouds pealed with thunder.
    Back and forth your lightning flew.

The wheel of your chariot thundered;
   The lightning lit up the world.
      The earth rumbled and roared.
You traveled along the sea;
   Your path was upon the great ocean.
      You left no footprint behind you.
By the hand of Moses and Aaron,
   You led your people like sheep.

PSALM 78

Listen, my people, to my teaching;
   Turn your ears to what my mouth says.
I will open my mouth to say something wise,
   And pour out hints from ancient times.
Things we heard, and now declare,
   Things our parents told to us—
Not keeping secrets from us, their descendants,
   Telling them to a new generation.
They told the glorious power of God,
   The amazing things the Lord has done;
The Lord, who made an agreement with Jacob,
   And gave instruction to Israel.
God wanted our parents to teach us
   All the commands they were given,
So the children they bore, the next generation,
   Might come to know these things.
They rose up and spoke to us, their children,
   And put their own faith in God.
They didn't forget God's deeds;
   They obeyed the Lord's commands.
They were not like their own forebears—
   An obstinate, stubborn generation.
A generation with no set purpose,
   Their spirit infirm in relation to God.
The tribe of Ephraim, armed with their bows,
   Who fled on the day of battle!
They had not kept God's covenant;
   They refused to walk by God's teaching.

They forgot the things the Lord had done,
    The wonders God had revealed to them.
The marvel performed for our ancestors,
    On the delta plains in the land of Egypt.
God split the sea and led them through,
    Between the waters that stood like a dam.
God led them by day from a cloud,
    And all night, from a blazing fire,
Cleaving huge rocks in the desert,
    Supplying water from deep underground.
God produced springs from the rock,
    And water poured out in streams.
And the people sinned yet again,
    Resisting almighty God in the desert!
They resolved to put God to the test,
    By selfishly asking for food.
They spoke out against God: "Could any god
    Provide us a feast in the desert?
God produced water by striking a rock,
    And making the streams pour out;
But how can God give us bread,
    Or provide enough meat for us all?"
God heard, and burned with anger toward Jacob;
    The wrath of the Lord flared up against Israel,
Because they had no faith in God,
    And did not trust their savior.
So God ordered meal from on high,
    And opened the cosmic doors.
God made it rain manna for them to eat,
    Giving them grain from the sky.
Each person ate food in abundance;
    God provided them more than enough.
When the east wind burst out of the sky,
    And the south wind came up by God's power,
Then meal rained on them like dust,
    And flying birds, like the sand of the sea.
Food fell in the midst of their camp,
    And all around their tents;
And they ate, until they could eat no more.
    God had brought them what they had desired.

And still their greed was unsatisfied,
  Though their mouths were stuffed with food.
And the wrath of the Lord flared up against them;
  God killed them in their portly pride,
    And forced their strong men to their knees,
In spite of all this, they continued to sin,
  And not to believe in God's miracles.
They ended their lives in futility,
  And approached their death with terror.
While people were dying, they sought the Lord;
  They turned back and inquired for God.
They recalled that the Lord was their mountain stronghold;
  Their redeemer, the Most High God.
But their mouths spoke only deception;
  Their lips were lying to God.
Their hearts were not set on the Lord,
  And they were untrue to God's covenant.
Yet God was compassionate, pardoning sin,
  Unwilling that they should be destroyed.
Again and again God's wrath was forestalled;
  The Lord refused to respond in anger,
Recalling that they were mortal flesh;
  Their spirit leaves and does not return.
How stubborn they were in the wilderness;
  How they offended God in the desert!
They put God to the test again and again,
  Provoking Israel's Holy One!
They failed to remember the hand of God,
  The day of their release from oppression—
The signs God sent against Egypt,
  The omens of God on the delta plains.
God changed the Nile into blood—
  They could not drink from their streams.
God sent voracious insects against them,
  And frogs that ruined their land.
God gave their harvest to locusts,
  Their produce to locust swarms.
God killed their vines with hail,
  Their fig trees with crushing storms.

Their cattle were overpowered by hail,
  Their flocks by lightning flame.
You sent against them your burning rage—
  Anger, and curse, and peril,
    A band of heralds of evil;
You cleared a path for your rage—
  Refusing to spare them from death,
    Resigning their lives to the plague.
You killed all Egypt's eldest sons,
  The pride and strength of the tents of Ham.
You led out your people like sheep,
  Guiding them like a flock in the desert;
Leading them without fear to safety,
  While the sea submerged their foes.
You brought them to your sacred mountain,
  The mountain made by your right hand.
You drove the nations out before them,
  And allotted a place for them;
    You settled Israel's tribes in their tents.
Yet they stubbornly put the High God to the test;
  They refused to heed God's warnings.
They returned to their ancestors' faithless ways,
  Like a warped and useless bow.
They offended God with their hilltop shrines;
  With their idols they made God jealous.
God understood, and was angry,
  And completely rejected Israel,
Abandoning Shiloh's tabernacle,
  The tent of God's presence among the people.
The ark of power God sent into exile;
  The hand of the enemy seized God's glory.
God gave up the people to slaughter;
  God rejected the land in anger.
Fire consumed their young men;
  The young women expressed no grief.
Their priests were felled by the sword;
  The widows wept no tears.
The Lord awoke as though from a stupor,
  Like someone recovering from wine,

And attacked the rear of the enemy,
  Disgracing them for all time to come.
But God still rejected the family of Joseph,
  And did not choose the tribe of Ephraim.
Instead, God chose the tribe of Judah
  And the mountain beloved by God—Mount Zion.
There God built the towering temple,
  Destined to last as long as the world.
And God elected David to serve there,
  Rather than tending sheep in their pens;
To shepherd Jacob, the people of God,
    Israel who is God's heritage,
      Rather than tending sheep and lambs.
And David did so, with all his heart;
  With skillful hands he guided them.

PSALM 79

God, the nations invade your heritage;
  They have defiled your holy temple,
    And left Jerusalem ruined.
They gave your servants' bodies,
  The flesh of your saints, to be food
    For beasts and flying birds.
They poured out blood like water;
  Around Jerusalem the dead lay unburied.
We are scorned by our neighbors,
  Humiliated by those around us.
Lord, will you be angry forever?
  How long will your zeal burn like fire?
Pour out your wrath on the nations,
  On those who do not know you,
    On the kingdoms that do not call you by name!
For they are devouring Jacob,
  Making his homeland a desolate waste.
Do not recall our former guilt;
  Bring your compassion quickly—
    For we are utterly helpless.
Save us, our rescuing God,
  That you may be rightly honored.

Save us and forgive us our sins,
  In accord with your true nature.
Why should the nations say, "Where is their God?"
  For your servants' blood that they poured out,
    Let them know your revenge, and let us see it happen!
Let the prisoner's groan come before you;
  May your power set free those condemned to die!
The scorn with which they scorned you, Lord,
  Heap into their own laps seven times over!
Let us be your people, the sheep you tend;
  And we will praise you forever,
    Reciting your praises age after age.

PSALM 80

Shepherd of Israel, listen;
  Lead Joseph as a flock.
You are enthroned on the cherubim;
  Shine on Ephraim, Benjamin, Manasseh.
Rouse yourself in your power,
  And come to rescue us.
God, restore us and help us,
  And let your face shine brightly.

Lord of the armies of earth and sky,
  How long will you fume while your people pray?
Will you feed us tears for bread,
  And make us drink gallons of tears?
You make us fight with our neighbors,
  And our enemies ridicule us.
God of heaven and earth, restore us;
  Let your face shine brightly, and help us.

You uprooted a vine from Egypt;
  You drove out nations to plant it.
You cleared a space for it;
  It rooted, and filled the land.
Its shadow hid the mountains;
  And its branches, the tallest cedars.
Its boughs grew out to the sea;
  And its shoots, to the river Euphrates.

Why have you torn down its wall,
   That all who pass by may pluck it?
The boar from the forest ravages it;
   The field rodents gnaw at it.
God of the armies of earth and sky,
   Look down from the heavens, and see!
Return to tend this vine,
   Here where your right hand planted it.
Burned by fire, cut down,
   It dies from your angry look.
Empower the king who rules in your name;
   He is mortal, but make him mighty.
Let us not be disloyal to you;
   Let us live! We appeal to you;
Lord of heaven and earth, restore us;
   Let your face shine brightly, and help us.

PSALM 81

Shout in joy to God, our strength;
   Shout aloud to Jacob's God!
Lift up a song; beat the tambourine.
   Make beautiful music with harp and lyre.
Sound the trumpet this holy day,
   For this our new moon festival.
For this is the custom in Israel,
   A command from Jacob's God,
Who established this sign for Joseph's people
   When they came out of Egypt.

"I heard your voice, though you were a stranger;
   I lifted the burden from your backs.
Your hands were freed from their toil;
   When you cried in distress, I saved you.
Unseen, I answered with thunder;
   I tested you at the spring of Meribah:

"Listen, my people, and I will instruct you;
   Israel, you must hear what I say.
Let there be no strange god among you;
   To a foreign god, do not bow down.

I, the Lord, am your God,
  Who brought you up from the land of Egypt.
    Open your mouths, and I will fill them.

"But my people refused to hear my voice;
  You, Israel, would not accept me.
I abandoned you to your own stubborn will—
  You just went on by your own designs.

"If only my people would listen to me,
  If only Israel walked in my ways,
How quickly I would subdue their foes,
  And turn my power against their oppressors!
They hate me, yet they pretend to serve me,
  With boundless perversity.
Yet I fed them with the finest grain,
  And satisfied them with the sweetest honey."

PSALM 82

Standing before the divine assembly,
  The Lord declares judgment among the gods:
"How long will you judge unjustly,
  And show favor to those who do wrong?
Be just to the poor and the orphan;
  Take the side of the wretched and needy!
Rescue the poor and oppressed
  From the power of evil people!
Don't you know what you're doing?
  Have you no understanding?
Will you keep on walking in darkness
  Until earth's foundations are shaken?
I have told you that you are gods,
  All of you, children of God on high;
But now you will die like mortals,
  And fall like some petty tyrant."
Rise up, O God, judge the world;
  Take sole possession of every land!

PSALM 83

God, you should not be resting!
  God, do not be deaf, or idle!
Don't you notice the din of your foes?
  Those who hate you are so defiant!
They plot against your nation,
  Conspiring against the people you treasure,
Saying, "Come, we will wipe them out as a people;
  Let Israel's name be remembered no more!"
United in purpose, they counsel and covenant;
  They have formed an alliance against you—
The tents of Edom, the Ishmaelites,
  Moab, and Hagar's descendants,
Byblos and Ammon, Amalekite tribes,
  Those who live in Philistia and Tyre.
Even Assyria joins with them—
  Arms and hands for Lot's descendants.
Do with them as you did with Midian,
  With Sisera and Jabin, at Qishon River!
They were destroyed at Endor;
  They became lumps of earth.
Their heroes were fed to the crows and wolves;
  Their leaders became like Zebach and Zalmuna—
They said, "We will dispossess for ourselves
  The place where God is living."
Make them, my God, like tumbleweed,
  Like chaff dispersed by the wind;
Be like the fire that burns the forest,
  Like the flame that devours the hills.
Drive them before your mighty wind;
  Terrify them with your storms.
Stuff contempt down their throats,
  Until they seek to know you, O Lord!
Let them be ever ashamed and afraid;
  Let them die in disgrace,
Until they admit that your name is Lord,
  That you alone are High God of the world.

PSALM 84

How beautiful is your home,
  Lord of the forces of earth and sky.
My inmost self longs and pines
  For the temple courts of the Lord.
My mind and body would sing for you,
  To you, the living God!
Even the birds can find a house.
  There is a nest for the swallows,
    Where they may place their young.
Oh that I might come to your altars,
  Lord of the forces of earth and sky;
    You are my sovereign God.
Happy are those who live in your house,
  Those who constantly praise you.
Happy are those who are strong in you;
  Your ways are in their hearts.
They travel through verdant valleys;
  God lets them drink from springs of water,
    And lets the rain fall gently around them.
They go from triumph to triumph;
  They look upon God in Zion.

Lord God of the forces of earth and sky,
  Hear my prayer and listen;
    You are Jacob's God.
Watch over our sovereign, O God;
  Be gracious to your Messiah.
Better one day in the courts of your temple
  Than a thousand days outside.
Better to beg at the door of God's house
  Than to live in the tents of oppressors.
For the Lord is our sovereign and sun;
  God is our wealth and our joy.
The Lord ungrudgingly gives good things
  To those who walk in the perfect way.
Lord of the forces of earth and sky,
  Happy are those who trust in you!

PSALM 85

Be kind to your land, O Lord;
   Bring to an end Jacob's exile.
Remove the guilt of your people;
   Forgive them all their sins.
Stop being angry with us,
   Turn away from your fiery wrath.
Restore us, our saving God,
   And cease to rage against us.
Will you fume at us forever,
   Staying angry, age after age?
If only you would restore us to life,
   And let your people rejoice in you!
Show us your constant love, O Lord,
   And offer us your salvation.

Let me hear what God declares,
   For the Lord is declaring peace:
"I tell the people devoted to me,
   Do not be complacent again!
For those who fear me, salvation is near;
   My glory will dwell in your land."
Devotion and faith join together;
   Peace and justice exchange a kiss.
Fidelity sprouts from the earth,
   And justice looks down from the sky.
Surely the Lord will send rain,
   And our land will produce the harvest.
Justice will come from God's presence,
   And beauty will follow justice.

PSALM 86

Listen, Lord, and answer me,
   For I am oppressed and poor.
Protect my life, for I am faithful;
   Save me, your servant, who trusts in you.
Be gracious to me, O Lord,
   For I call to you all day long.

Let me, your servant, live in joy,
　　For to you, my sovereign, I offer my life.
For you, O Lord, are kind and forgiving,
　　Completely faithful to all who call you.
Listen, O Lord, to my prayer;
　　Attend to the sound of my cry for help.
In the day of distress I call to you,
　　For you will respond to me.
There is none like you among the gods;
　　Lord, no one can do what you have done.
All the nations, whom you have made,
　　Will come and bow before you;
　　　　Lord, they will honor your name.
For you are great, and do marvelous things;
　　You alone are God.
Teach me your way, O Lord;
　　I will walk by faith in you.
　　　　To fear your name is my only goal.
I will praise my Lord God with all my heart,
　　And will honor your name forever.
Your constant love for me is so great;
　　You snatched me away from death's deep realm.
O God, the arrogant rise against me;
　　A violent mob is trying to kill me.
　　　　They pay no attention to you!
But you are a gracious, compassionate God,
　　So slow to be angry, determined to love us.
　　　　Pay attention to me, and be gracious.
Give your strength to me, your servant;
　　Save me, the child of a woman who served you.
Do something with me that shows your goodness,
　　The sight of which will shame those who hate me.
　　　　You help me and comfort me, Lord.

PSALM 87

Established among the holy hills,
　　Zion's gates, you are loved by the Lord
　　　　More than any of Jacob's shrines.

What marvels are spoken concerning you,
    By the God whose city you are:
"I make Egypt and Babylon recognize me,
    Along with Philistia, Cush, and Tyre,
        As though they all were born here."
But of Zion it will be said:
    "Each of these people was born within her;
        The High God keeps her secure."
The Lord will write in the list of nations:
    "This is the people born here,"
And all who have suffered because they lived here
    Will finally dance and sing.

PSALM 88

O Lord, my saving God,
    By day I cry out;
        At night I am in your presence.
Let my prayer come before you;
    Listen when I shout.
I have had all I can take of evil;
    They are beating me to death.
I am reckoned among the dying,
    Like a man whose strength is gone.
To death I am given over,
    Like someone stabbed with a sword,
        Like those who lie in the grave.
There you no longer recall them;
    They are cut off from your power.
You put me far underground, in a pit,
    In a dark place of deep recesses.
Your anger weighs upon me,
    Subduing me like waves from the sea.
You make my acquaintances stay far away;
    You make me abhorrent to them.
I stay indoors; I never go out.
    I am going blind with despair.
Every day I call to you, Lord;
    I reach out my hands to you.

Have you worked a marvel among the dead—
    Will the ghosts rise up to praise you?
Is your constant love discussed in the grave?
    Is your faithfulness known in the nether world?
Is your marvelous work understood in the darkness,
    Your justice in the Land of Forgetting?
I cry to you for help, O Lord;
    At dawn my prayer comes before you.
Why reject me, O Lord?
    Why hide your face from me?
I have been wretched and weary since childhood;
    I have lived in fear of your anger.
Your burning wrath sweeps over me;
    Your horrors render me speechless.
They engulf me like water all day long;
    They utterly overwhelm me.
You keep me far from my closest companion;
    You deprive me of neighbors and friends.

PSALM 89

The grace of the Lord is eternal—
    I sing for the ages to come;
        My mouth declares your truth.
I know you, O Ancient God;
    The skies were built by your grace,
        And your truth is established on high.
"I covenant with my chosen one,
    I swear to David my servant:
I secure your line for all time;
    I establish your throne for ages to come."

Your deed will be praised in the skies, O Lord;
    And your truth in the saints' assembly.
The skies will praise your work, O Lord;
    The angels' assembly will praise your truth.
For who in heaven compares with the Lord?
    What divine being can equal our God?
A God so awesome among all the gods,
    So greatly feared by all your attendants!

Lord of victory, who is like you?
  Mighty Lord, surrounded by truth!
You rule the depths of the sea;
  You calm the surging waves.
You crush the sea serpent's carcass;
  Your mighty arm scatters your foes.
To you belong the earth and the sky;
  You laid the inhabited world's foundations.
You created the hemispheres;
  The highest mountains praise your name.
You are the one with the mighty arm;
  Your strong right hand is lifted high.
Your throne is founded on justice and right;
  Your attendants, O God, are grace and truth.
Happy the people who heed your summons;
  They march, O Lord, in the light of your presence.
All day long they shout your name,
  And boast of your justice triumphant.
For you are their splendid power;
  By your grace, their heads are held high.
For you, O Lord, are our sovereign;
  You, Israel's Holy One, rule us.
Long ago you spoke through the seer,
  And addressed your faithful people!
"I lift up a young man from among you,
  To be your helper and hero.
I have found my servant David,
  And anointed him as Messiah.
He will be secure in my hand;
  Surely my arm will strengthen him.
No foes will ever outwit him;
  Nor will treacherous people subdue him.
I smash his oppressors before him;
  I strike down people who hate him.
My constant love is with him;
  His pride is in knowing me.
I place the seas in his control;
  His right hand rules the rivers.
He calls to me: 'You are my father;
  My God and my mountain refuge!'

I give him a son and heir—
　The greatest king in the world.
Forever will I protect him,
　Secure in my steadfast covenant.
His dynasty is eternal;
　I will make his throne outlast the skies.
And should his descendants abandon my teaching,
　Refusing to walk by my commands,
If they profane my decrees,
　And disobey my orders,
My rod will take care of their revolt;
　They will reckon their sins by their bruises.
But never will I put an end to my love,
　Nor deny my faithful promise to David.
My covenant I will never renounce,
　Nor prevent the words my lips have spoken.
I swore in my holiness this one thing—
　I will never be false to David.
His line will go on forever;
　His throne will shine as long as the sun,
Just like the moon, established forever,
　Secured, like the skies, for all time."

But you have scorned your Messiah,
　Rejecting him in your anger,
Disavowing your servant's covenant,
　Desecrating his royal crown.
You tore down all his walls of defense,
　And left his fortresses in ruins.
Every passerby plunders him,
　And all his neighbors despise him.
You make his opponents mighty,
　And fill his foes with joy.
You deflect the blade of his sword,
　And do not sustain him in battle.
You put an end to his splendor,
　And throw down his throne to the ground.
You have made him old before his time;
　You have wrapped him in shame like a cloak.

"How long, O Lord? Will you hide forever?

Must your anger burn like fire?
Remember how short my life will be;
  Have you created us all for nothing?
Who can live, and never know death,
  Or save their own lives from the grave?
Where is your former commitment, Lord,
  That you so firmly swore to David?
Notice, O Lord, your servant's disgrace—
  How I bear in my breast all these pagan arrows;
While all your foes are mocking me,
  Mocking and slandering your anointed."

[Blessed be the Lord forever!
  Amen and amen.]

PSALM 90

Lord, you have been a home for us,
  For one generation after another.
Before the mountains were born,
  Before you gave birth to the continents,
    All through the ages you were God.
You turn everyone back into dust;
  You say, "Return, you mortal creatures!"
For in your eyes a thousand years
  Are like yesterday when it is gone,
    Like keeping watch for a night.
Our life begins in sleep;
  At dawn we sprout like grass.
At dawn we blossom and sprout;
  At evening we dry up and wither away.
For we are destroyed by your anger,
  And quickly dispatched by your rage.
You bring out our sins where you can see them;
  Your presence lights up our shameful secrets.
Every day we feel your wrath;
  We finish our years with sighing.
Our lives may go on for seventy years,
  Or even for eighty, if we are strong;
    But those years are nothing but work and pain.

Who understands your mighty anger,
  The rage that makes us afraid of you?
Teach us how to plan our days,
  And let our conduct be wise.
Repent, O Lord! How long will this last?
  Be gracious to us, your servants.
Kindly care for us each morning;
  All our lives let us sing for joy.
Delight us as long as you have oppressed us,
  As many years as we have seen trouble.
Let your work be plain to your servants,
  And show our children your splendor.
Let our God's kindness rest upon us,
  And let the work we have done endure.
    What our hands have done—let it endure!

PSALM 91

You live in God's secret place;
  The Most High shades your sleep.
You say to the Lord, "My strong refuge,
  My God, in whom I trust."
God saves you from fowlers' snares,
  And from deadly disease.
The Lord's pinions are over you;
  You hide beneath God's wings.
Do not fear the terror of night,
  Or the arrow that flies by day,
The pestilence stalking in darkness,
  The plague laying waste at noon.
A thousand may fall at your side,
  Ten thousand at your right hand;
But you will not be stricken—
  The faithful God is your shield and tower.
Only look with your eyes,
  And see the oppressors punished.
As for you, the Lord is your refuge;
  You have made the Most High your shelter.
Evil will not befall you,
  Nor harm approach your tent.

On your behalf, God commanded the angels
　To guard you in all your ways.
Their hands will lift you high,
　Lest you catch your foot on a stone.
You shall step on lion and snake,
　Tread down young lion and serpent.
"I will save those who cling to me,
　And protect those who know my name.
They call and I answer them;
　I am with them in their distress.
I will rescue them and reward them;
　I satisfy them with long life,
　　And show them my saving power."

PSALM 92

It is good to praise you, Lord,
　And to sing to your name, O God on high,
Proclaiming each morning that you are faithful,
　Each evening that we can trust in you,
Using ten-stringed lyre and harp,
　Using the sounds of music.
Lord, you have made me delight in your actions;
　I celebrate what your hands have done.
How great are your deeds, O Lord!
　Your intentions are so mysterious!
Some people are stupid like cattle,
　Too foolish to see what you are doing
When evil people shoot up like weeds
　And wrongdoers seem to sprout everywhere,
Only to be wiped out for all time,
　While you, Lord, are lifted high forever.
Right now, O Lord, your foes are dying,
　And all who do wrong are scattered.
But you make me as strong as an ox,
　And pour luxuriant oils on me.
I can see what my foes are doing—
　I hear that cruel people are rising against me;

But the one who does right will bloom like a palm,
   And grow tall like a Lebanon cedar.
Planted within the Lord's own house,
   They bloom in the courts of our God.
We prosper even when we grow old;
   We are healthy and flourishing,
Declaring that God is reliable,
   My rock, in whom there is no flaw.

PSALM 93

The Lord reigns, robed in splendor;
   Clothe yourself, O Lord, in power!
Truly you have established the world;
   Never will it totter.
Your throne has long been firmly placed;
   You have existed since time began.

Lord, the rivers call out,
   The rivers call out with their voices;
      The rivers call out with their pounding roar.
You, Lord, so high above,
   Are stronger than crashing waves on the sea,
      Than the sound of many waterfalls.
Your instructions are so reliable;
   Your beautiful house is so holy;
      You are the Lord to the end of time.

PSALM 94

The God of judgment is the Lord;
   The God of judgment shines like the sun.
Rise up, O ruler of all the world;
   Treat the proud as they treated others!
Lord, how long will the wicked go on?
   How long will the wicked celebrate wildly?
They bubble over with insolent speech;
   Plotting with others as evil as they are.

They crush your people to dust, O Lord,
    And humiliate those who belong to you.
They murder the widows and aliens;
    They slaughter those who are orphans.
They say, "The Lord will never notice;
    Jacob's God will pay no attention."

Look here, you who consume other people—
    When will you look at your own stupid pride?
Won't the God who made ears overhear you?
    Won't the eye's inventor be able to see?
The One who taught all people to know,
    Who disciplines nations, will surely judge!
The Lord understands all human designs—
    They are only a passing breath.
Happy are those you discipline, Lord;
    To whom you teach your will,
That they may have peace after perilous times,
    After the wicked have dug their own graves!
For you will not forsake your people,
    Nor abandon those who belong to you.
For justice is done to those who are just;
    There are consequences for those who do right!

Who stands with me against the oppressors?
    Who will confront the wicked with me?
If the Lord were not my helper,
    I would soon inhabit a quiet grave!
Instead, when I say, "I am falling, Lord!",
    Your constant love sustains me.
Disquieting thoughts may crowd my mind,
    But then your consoling presence caresses me.
Powers of chaos can't magically bind you,
    Nor works of evil defy your decree.
They band together to murder the righteous,
    Condemning innocent people to death—
But the Lord became a fortress for me;
    My God is my rock of refuge.
Their own misdeeds will turn against them;
    God will silence them in their scheming.
        The Lord our God will silence them.

PSALM 95

Come, let us sing to the Lord;
  Let us shout to our saving rock!
Enter God's presence with praise,
  With music and shouts of joy.
For the Lord is a mighty God,
  The great ruler of all the gods.
God's hand holds the depths of the world,
  And rules the peaks of the mountains.
It is God who made and rules the seas,
  Whose hand created dry ground.
Come, let us kneel and worship the Lord;
  Let us bow before God our maker.
Today God will be our God—
  Who chooses a people and tends them,
Whose hand will guide us like sheep—
  If you will only heed God's voice:
"Do not harden your hearts as you did at Meribah—
  As you did at Massah in the desert.
There your ancestors put me on trial;
  Having seen my power, they tested me still!
For forty years I despised them all—
  I saw how weak-willed they were
Because they ignored my ways,
  I swore in my anger to give them no rest."

PSALM 96

Sing a new song to the Lord;
  Sing to the Lord, all the world.
Sing and bless the name of the Lord;
  Proclaim God's salvation, day after day.
Speak of God's glory among the nations,
  Of wonders from God among all peoples.
For the Lord is great, much to be praised,
  More fearful than all other gods.

For the nations' gods are worthless things,
 But the Lord has made the sky.
Majestic and grand is God's presence;
 Strength and splendor are in God's temple.
Give to the Lord, you tribes and peoples,
 Give to the Lord glory and strength.
Give the glory the Lord deserves;
 Bring a gift and come to God's court.
Bow to the Lord in holy splendor;
 Tremble before God, all the world.
Say to the nations, "The Lord will reign,
 Establishing lands that never will totter!"
Let sky and earth rejoice and shout;
 Thunder, you sea and everything in you!
Let the desert and everything in it rejoice;
 Let all the trees of the forest sing
Before the Lord, who comes,
 Who comes to rule the world,
Who rules the earth with justice,
 Faithfully judging the peoples.

PSALM 97

The Lord reigns; let the earth rejoice!
 Let the many coastlands celebrate!
Clouds and storm surround the Lord,
 Whose throne is founded on justice and right.
The Lord sends out fiery flames,
 Searing enemies all around.
God's lightning bolts light up the world;
 The earth will see, and tremble in fear.
Mountains will melt like wax
 Before the Lord of all the earth,
Whose righteousness the skies declare,
 Whose glory is seen by all the peoples.
The idol-worshippers all are ashamed—
 They have boasted in insignificant things;
  Now all gods bow down to the Lord.

Zion will hear of this and rejoice,
    And Judah's towns will celebrate,
        Because of your judgments, Lord.
For you are indeed the Lord,
    High above all the world,
        Exalted high above all the gods.
Lord, you love those who hate evil,
    And guard the lives of your loyal people;
        You save them from the oppressors' power.

Light shines out for the righteous person;
    There is joy for those whose will is justice.
Rejoice in the Lord, you who are righteous;
    Praise the holy name of the Lord.

PSALM 98

Sing a new song to the Lord,
    Who has done such marvelous things,
Whose right hand and holy arm
    Have come to rescue me.

Lord, you made known your saving power;
    You revealed to the nations your justice.
You remembered your faithful love,
    For all your family Israel.
The farthest ends of the world
    Have seen our God's saving power.

Shout to the Lord, every land!
    Be confident! Shout and sing!
Sing to the Lord with a harp,
    With a harp and the sound of music!
With sounding horns and trumpets,
    Shout to the Lord, the King!

Storm, you ocean, and all that fills you,
    You lands, and all who inhabit you.
Clap your hands, great rivers;
    You hills, all shout together

Before the Lord, who comes,
  Who comes to rule the world,
To rule the lands with justice
  And rightly govern the peoples.

PSALM 99

The Lord reigns; let the nations tremble!
  God's throne is the cherubim; let the earth shake!
The Lord is far above Mount Zion,
  And high above all nations;
They praise you, great and fearful Lord,
  For you, O God, are holy.
The strength of a king is his love of justice—
  You, O God, have established order;
True justice is done among Jacob's descendants—
  God, this is your doing!
Let us lift up our Lord on high,
  And bow down at the footstool of God.
Moses and Aaron are among the Lord's priests,
  And Samuel, too, calls God by name.
They call to the Lord who answers them,
  Who speaks to them from a pillar of cloud.
They obeyed your decrees, the orders you gave them;
  Lord our God, you have answered them.
You have been a forgiving God to them,
  Yet you punished them for their unworthy deeds.
Let us lift up our Lord on high,
  And bow down at the holy mountain of God;
    For the Lord our God is holy.

PSALM 100

Shout to the Lord, all the land;
  Serve the Lord with joy;
    Come before God with laughter.
Know that the Lord is God;

We belong to the Lord our maker,
   To God, who tends us like sheep.
Come to God's gates with thanks;
   Come to God's courts with praise;
     Praise and bless the Lord's name.
Truly the Lord is good;
   God is always gracious,
     And faithful age after age.

PSALM 101

I, the king, praise justice and love;
   I sing to you, O Lord.
I devote myself to your perfect way—
   When will you come to me?
I conduct myself with pure intent
   Among those of my royal household.
I never allow any worthless thing
   To come before my eyes.
I hate illusion and treachery;
   They will not hold on to me!
Leave me, you with perverted wills;
   I don't wish to know evil people.
Those who secretly slander their friends
   Are people whom I will silence!
Those who are proud and ambitious—
   I cannot endure them!
I look for faithful citizens;
   They will dwell with me.
Those who intend to do what is best
   Will be the ones who serve me.
No one will live in my royal household
   Who does anything deceitful.
Those who lie will not be allowed
   To remain here in my sight.
I, the king, will silence like cattle
   All in this land who do evil,
Cutting off from the Lord's own city
   All who do what is wrong.

PSALM 102

Hear my prayer, O Lord;
　Let my cry for help come to you.
Do not hide your face from me
　In the day of my distress.
Turn your ear to me;
　The day I call, hurry to answer me.
For my days disappear like smoke,
　As though flames consumed my body.
Like grass, my heart is so beaten and withered
　That I have forgotten to eat my food.
The sound of my groaning wearies me;
　My bones are stuck to my skin.
I am like an owl in the wild,
　Like a little owl in a desert;
Keeping watch all alone,
　Like a bird perched on a rooftop.
All day my enemies taunt me;
　Trying to drive me insane.
So I eat dust for my food,
　And mix my drink with tears.
How can I face your angry curse!
　You raised me only to throw me down.
Each day stretches out like a shadow,
　And I am withered like grass.
But you, Lord, will last forever,
　Famous down through the ages.
Raise up Mount Zion in mercy—
　The appointed time of grace has come!
For your servants delight in her stones,
　And pity even her dust.
Then the nations will fear the Lord's name,
　And earth's kings will be awed by your glory.
For the Lord is the builder of Zion;
　There God will appear in splendor.
God attends to the prayers of the naked;
　Their prayers God does not despise.
Write this down for the next generation;
　Those not yet created will praise the Lord.

For the Lord looks down from the holy height;
   From the sky God scans the world,
To hear the groan of those in prison
   To free those condemned to death,
That they may declare the Lord's name in Zion,
   And praise their God in Jerusalem,
When peoples are gathered together
   And nations, to serve the Lord.
But I have no strength for the journey;
   My days are too short—speak to me!
Don't take me away after half a life—
   You whose years go on through the ages.
You were there when the earth was founded;
   The skies are the work of your hands.
They will perish, but you will endure;
   They will all wear out like garments.
You will change them as though they were clothes,
   But you are the one whose years do not end.
Let your servants' descendants survive,
   And their offspring remain in your presence.

PSALM 103

Bless the Lord, my inmost self!
   Everything in me, bless God's holy name.
Bless the Lord, my inmost self,
   Do not forget what God has done—
Pardoning all your sin,
   Healing your every disease,
Redeeming your life from the grave,
   Crowning your head with constant compassion.
Your vital needs are satisfied;
   Like the phoenix, your youth is renewed.
The Lord accomplishes justice—
   Vindication for all the oppressed!
God's ways were made known to Moses,
   God's acts to Israel's offspring.
Compassion and grace—that is the Lord,
   Slow to be angry, determined to love us!

God will not always oppose us,
  Nor hold a grudge forever.
God does not act in accord with our sins,
  Nor as our guilt deserves.
As high as the sky is above the world,
  So great is the grace given those who fear God.
As far as the east is from the west,
  God removes our offenses from us.
Like a father's love for his child
  Is the love shown to those who fear God.
Surely God knows how we were made,
  And recalls that we are dust!
Our human life is a reed,
  A flower that blooms in the meadow.
It is gone when the wind blows over it;
  Its place recalls it no more.
But the grace of the Lord is eternal,
  Resting forever on those who fear God.
God's justice belongs to their offspring,
  To all who keep the covenant;
    Who remember to do what God commands.
The Lord has set a throne in the sky;
  God's authority governs all things.
Divine messengers, bless the Lord,
  Mighty heroes, doing God's word,
    And hearing the word God speaks.
Divine warriors, bless the Lord,
  Servants who do whatever God pleases.
All you creatures, bless the Lord
  Whose dominion is everywhere.
    Bless the Lord, my inmost self!

PSALM 104

Bless the Lord, my inmost self;
  O Lord, my God, you are very great.
You are clothed in majestic splendor;
  Light covers you like a garment.

You stretched out the sky like a tent,
    Extending the roof high over the waters.
Have you not made the clouds your chariot,
    Riding the wings of the wind?
You make the winds your messengers;
    Your servants, a blazing fire.
You set the earth upon its foundations;
    It will not totter for ages to come.
You clothed the world with the sea,
    Casting water over the hills.
But the waters fled when you rebuked them;
    They quickly withdrew at the sound of your thunder.
Mountains rose and valleys sank
    To the levels you had assigned them.
And you set limits the seas cannot cross;
    They cannot return to cover the world.
Yet don't you also send springs through channels,
    Making them run among the hills?
The springs provide water for animals,
    And satisfy thirsty beasts.
The birds of the sky alight around them,
    Singing among the bushes and shrubs.
You water even the summits of hills;
    You satisfy earth with the fruits of your work.
You make grass sprout for the cattle,
    And plants to meet human needs,
Bringing bread out of the ground,
    And wine to cheer our hearts,
Making our faces shine with oil,
    Giving strength to our hearts with food.
You sustain the trees of the wilderness,
    The cedars you planted in Lebanon,
Where songbirds make their nests,
    And the herons live in the treetops.
The heights of the mountains are homes for wild goats,
    And the rocks are shelter for badgers.
You make the moon measure out the seasons,
    And tell the sun when to rise.
You bring the darkness, and it is night,
    And the wild beasts creep through the thickets—

Lions roaring in search of their prey,
  Seeking their food from God.
But you gather them in at sunrise,
  And they lie down in their dens.
Then the people go out to work,
  To labor until the evening.

How many things you have made, O Lord!
  And you shaped every one in wisdom.
    The world is full of your creatures.
For instance, the great and spacious sea—
  There are the swarms beyond counting
    Of creatures both large and small.
There is the whale you formed,
  To play while ships go to and fro.
All these creatures wait for you
  To give them food at the proper times.
They gather what you provide;
  You open your hand and they are well-fed.
You hide your face; they are terrified!
  You stop their breath, and they die;
    And then they return to dust.
You send your spirit and they are created;
  The face of the earth is renewed.

May God's glory go on forever!
  Rejoice, O Lord, in what you have made!
You look down at the earth and it trembles;
  You strike the mountains and make them smoke.
I will sing to the Lord as long as I live;
  I will sing to my God with all my might.
I am happy to think of God;
  I am filled with joy in the Lord.
The sinners will all be removed from this world;
  Oppressors will be no more.
Bless the Lord, my inmost self;
  Praise the Lord! Hallelujah!

PSALM 105

Call on the name of the Lord in praise;
  Make known God's deeds among the nations.
Sing to God with joyful songs;
  Think of God's wonderful deeds!
Glory in God's holy name!
  You who seek the Lord, may your hearts rejoice.
Search for the might of the Lord;
  Constantly seek God's face.
Recall the wonders that God has performed,
  The warnings and judgments that God has spoken.
You offspring of Abraham, God's servant,
  You children of Jacob, God's chosen one,
This is the Lord, our God,
  Whose judgments fill the world.

God, remember your covenant always;
  Let your word direct a thousand generations.
Remember your promise to Abraham,
  The oath you swore to Isaac,
The decree you established for Jacob,
  Israel's lasting covenant:
You said, "I mark out your heritage;
  Canaan's land I give to you.
Your ancestors never were numerous;
  At first they were strangers here.
They wandered from country to country,
  One kingdom or people after another.
Yet no one ever oppressed them for long;
  No kings gained authority over them.
I forbade the nations to wrong my prophets,
  Or hurt the people I had anointed."

Then God decreed a worldwide famine,
  And every store of grain gave out.
God sent before the people a man,
  Joseph, sold to be a slave.
They bound his feet with fetters
  And shackled his neck with irons,

That the word of the Lord might test him with fire,
   Until God's purpose refined him like gold.
Then God sent a king who let Joseph go free,
   A ruler of nations who opened the prison.
The king made Joseph the lord of the palace,
   And steward of all the king's possessions.
To teach the princes to be like himself,
   To instruct his elders in wisdom.
And Israel came to live in Egypt;
   Jacob sojourned in Hamite lands.

The people of God were made fruitful;
   God made them outnumber the oppressors.
God made the Egyptians determined to hate them,
   And Egypt cruelly betrayed God's servants.
Then came Moses, the servant God sent,
   And Aaron, whom God had chosen.
They did great signs of God in Egypt;
   The Hamite land saw fearful portents.
God sent darkness, and all was black,
   But Egypt refused to hear God's word.
God changed their streams and pools to blood,
   And all their fish were killed.
God caused their land to teem with frogs,
   They even swarmed the king's private chambers.
God spoke, and the noxious insects appeared;
   Gnats were everywhere in the land.
Instead of rain, God sent them hail,
   The earth was struck by spears of lightning.
God struck down their vines and fig trees,
   And splintered every tree in the land.
God spoke, and the locusts appeared,
   So many that no one could count them.
They ate all that grew on the earth,
   They devoured the crops of Egypt's soil.
Then God struck down all the firstborn sons,
   The firstfruits of Egypt's vitality.

God's people carried out silver and gold;
   No one, from all their tribes, was in need.

Egypt rejoiced when the Hebrews departed;
  The Egyptians were terrified of them.
God spread out a cloud to cover them,
  And fire to brighten the night.
They asked, and God brought them quails;
  God fed them with food from the sky.
God opened the rock, and water flowed;
  A river streamed through the desert.
Lord, you recalled your holy word,
  Your oath to your servant Abraham.
You brought out your people, rejoicing;
  Your chosen ones came forth laughing.
You gave to them the lands of whole nations;
  They took the possessions of many peoples,
In order that they might obey your decrees,
  And learn to comply with your instruction.

Praise the Lord!
  Hallelujah!

PSALM 106

Sing praise to the Lord, who is good,
  Whose faithfulness lasts forever.
Can anyone tell all the Lord's mighty deeds,
  And make known the whole of God's praise?
Happy are those who do what is right,
  Who do justice all the time.
Remember me, Lord, when you bless your people;
  Care for me with your saving power—
Let me share the success of your chosen ones,
  And rejoice in the joy of your people,
    Among those who forever belong to you.

Along with our ancestors, we have sinned;
  Doing injustice, distorting your way.
Our ancestors, even in Egypt,
  Did not comprehend your wonders.
They forgot your great fidelity,
  Refusing to trust you beside the Red Sea.

And yet, to show who you are, you saved them,
  To demonstrate your power.
You rebuked the Red Sea, and it drained away;
  You led them through deeps as though through a desert.
You redeemed them from those who hated them,
  And saved them from the grip of their foes.
The waters buried their oppressors.
  Not a single one survived.
Then they trusted in your word;
  Then they sang your praise.
But how quickly they forgot your deeds,
  Impatient with your intentions.
In the wilderness they nursed their cravings,
  And tested you, O God, in the desert.
You gave to them what they asked,
  Freeing their stomachs from hunger.
When, in their tents, they envied Moses,
  And Aaron, the holy one of the Lord,
The earth opened up and swallowed Dathan,
  And buried the clan of Abiram.
Fire consumed their company,
  And flame devoured those wicked people.
And then, at Horeb, they made the calf,
  And bowed in worship before a statue.
They exchanged the God who was their glory,
  For the shape of a bull that feeds on hay.
They forgot the God who had rescued them,
  Who in Egypt had done such mighty deeds,
Such wonders in the land of Ham,
  Such terrors beside the Red Sea.
Then you decided to destroy them,
  Except for Moses, your chosen one.
But Moses defended them before you,
  To deflect your ruinous wrath.
Yet they rejected the land they desired,
  Refusing to trust your word.
They sulked in their tents, complaining,
  Ignoring your summons, O Lord.
You raised up your hand against them,

To fell them in the desert,
To drop them among the nations,
  To scatter them throughout the world.
They committed themselves to the idol of Peor,
  And offered sacrifice to the dead.
They offended you with their deeds,
  And the plague broke out among them.
Then Phineas stood up to pray,
  And the plague was brought to an end.
So Phineas is accounted righteous,
  With all his descendants, forevermore.
Then they angered you at the well of Meribah;
  Because of them, things went wrong for Moses.
For they had made him bitter in spirit,
  So that he railed with a reckless tongue.
They didn't exterminate the peoples,
  As you, O Lord, had told them to do.
Instead, they were mingled among the nations,
  And learned to imitate their deeds.
And so they began to serve the idols,
  And the idols became a snare for them.
They offered their sons in sacrifice,
  They gave their daughters to demons.
They shed the blood of innocent people,
  And with that blood they defiled the land.
By their acts they became unclean,
  And prostituted themselves by their deeds.
And your anger flared against your people;
  You loathed your special people, Lord!
You gave them into the hands of the nations;
  You let their foes rule over them.
Their enemies tormented them,
  And they were subdued by their power.
How many times you rescued them,
  But they kept on stubbornly disobeying,
    And sinking further into sin.
You had regard for their distress
  Whenever you heard their moaning cry,
Recalling your covenant with them,

Comforting them with great faithfulness.
You treated them with compassion,
　In the sight of all their oppressors.

Save us now, O Lord our God!
　Gather us from among the nations.
Let us praise your holy name;
　Let us glory in praising you,
Blessed be the Lord, who is Israel's God
　From time's beginning until its end.

[Let all the people say, "Amen! Hallelujah!"]

PSALM 107

Praise the Lord, who is good,
　Whose faithfulness lasts forever.
Let the redeemed confess that the Lord
　Redeemed them from the oppressor's power,
And gathered them from many lands—
　From east and west, north and south.
They wandered in wild deserted places
　Finding no way to a habitable city,
So weak with hunger and thirst
　That they lost their will to live.
They cried to the Lord in their distress;
　God rescued them from their sufferings,
Leading them by a level road
　Until they came to a habitable city.
Praise the Lord, who is faithful,
　Who works such wonders for mortals,
Who gives the thirsty plenty to drink,
　And fills the hungry with food.

Those who lived in darkness and shadows,
　Prisoners bound by need or by chains,
Who resisted the word of the Lord,
　And disdained the counsel of God Most High—
Burdened with toil, they had lost heart;
　They fell, and no one helped them up.

They cried to the Lord in their distress;
    God rescued them from their sufferings,
Bringing them out of darkness and shadows
    And tearing away their bonds.
Praise the Lord, who is faithful,
    Who works such wonders for mortals;
Who shattered the doors of bronze,
    And broke in pieces the iron bars.

Those tormented by guilt,
    Made fools by the power of sin—
They came to abhor their food,
    And arrived at the gates of death.
They cried to the Lord in their distress;
    God rescued them from their sufferings.
God sent word and healed them,
    Rescuing them from their ruinous ways.
Praise the Lord, who is faithful,
    Who works such wonders for mortals.
Bring thanksgiving offerings;
    Declare God's deeds with shouts of joy.

Those who go down to the ocean in ships,
    Who do their work on the open sea—
They have seen, out on the deep,
    The marvelous deeds of the Lord,
Who spoke, and the gale wind came,
    And the waves of the sea rose up.
The ships were tossed from the depths to the skies,
    And the sailors dissolved in misery;
They lurched and staggered as though they were drunk,
    And all their skill was lost in confusion.
They cried to the Lord in their distress;
    God rescued them from their sufferings.
The gale became calm and still;
    The waves of the sea were quiet.
The sailors rejoiced in the calm;
    God led them to their desired harbor.
Praise the Lord, who is faithful,
    Who works such wonders for mortals.

Let the congregation exalt the Lord,
    And the council of elders, sing praise to God.
God made oceans into deserts,
    And turned flowing springs into arid ground.
God made fruitful earth become barren,
    An evil place for those who lived there.
God made the desert a pool of water,
    And waterless land into flowing springs.
Then the hungry could live there;
    God established a habitable city.
They sowed their fields and planted vineyards,
    And made the fruit trees productive.
God blessed them, and they became numerous;
    Their flocks and herds increased.
Pouring contempt on tyrants,
    God sent them out into trackless wastes.
They, brought low, were diminished
    By cruel abuse and torment.
God protected the poor from affliction,
    And nurtured their families like lambs.

Those who do right will see and rejoice,
    The evil will shut their mouths.
Whoever is wise will treasure these things;
    God's faithful people will ponder them.

PSALM 108

Let my mind be resolute, God;
    Let me chant and sing with all my might.
Let my harp and lyre awaken;
    I will awaken the morning light.
I praise you, Lord, among the nations;
    I sing to you among the peoples.
Great beyond the sky is your love;
    Your faithfulness is above the clouds.
Arise beyond the sky, O God;
    Reveal your glory above all the world.
Thus will you save your beloved people;
    Your right hand will come down to save us.

God speaks from the sanctuary:
  "I proudly apportion Shechem;
    I measure the valley of Succoth.
Gilead and Manasseh are mine;
  Ephraim crowns my head;
    Judah becomes my royal scepter.
Moab is my basin for washing;
  Edom the mat where I toss my shoes.
    I triumph over the Philistines!"
Who will give us the fortified city?
  Who will bring us the throne of Edom?
God, have you not abandoned us?
  You don't go out with our armies!
Give us deliverance from our foes—
  For human aid is useless.
With God we will do a mighty deed;
  God will trample down our oppressors!

PSALM 109

God, whom I praise, do not be deaf!
  Evil and treacherous people
    Open their mouths against me.
They address me with lying tongues;
  Words of hate surround me,
    Attacking me for no reason.
They hate me, although I loved them,
  And prayed on their behalf.
They return me evil instead of good,
  Hatred instead of love.
Send the Evil One against them;
  Let the Avenger confront each one.
Find them guilty when they are judged;
  Reckon their prayers as sin.
Let their days be few;
  Let someone else possess their wealth.
Let their children be orphans;
  Let their wives be widows.

Let their children be wandering beggars
  Banished from their ruined homes.
Let creditors repossess all that they have;
  Let foreigners plunder their property.
Let no one show them any mercy;
  Let no one pity their orphans.
Let their descendants all be cut off;
  Blot out their name in the next generation.
But, Lord, remember their fathers' guilt;
  Do not blot out their mothers' sin.
Keep their wrongs forever before you,
  But let the world forget them completely.
For they forgot how to be faithful;
  They persecuted the helpless poor,
    And hounded to death the brokenhearted.
They loved to curse—and loved the results!
  They never wanted to bless—far from it!
Their curse they wore like a robe;
  It was the blood that flowed in their veins,
    The marrow within their bones.
So let them put on this garment;
  Let them always wear this sash.
Thus may the Lord reward my accusers,
  Those who speak evil trying to kill me.
But as for you, O Lord, my Lord,
  Treat me the way you have done before.
Save me, because you are faithful and good,
  For I am helpless and poor;
    My heart is wounded within me.
I pass away like a fading shadow;
  They brush me off like a locust.
My knees are unsteady from hunger;
  No fat is left on my body.
They think of me as disgraced;
  They see me and shake their heads.
Rescue me, O Lord my God;
  Save me because you love me.
Let them know that your hand has done it,
  That you, O Lord, have acted.

Let them curse—if you will bless;
  I can sing while they rise to mock me.
Clothe my accusers in shame;
  Let them wear their disgrace like a robe.
I will thank you out loud, over and over,
  And praise you, Lord, among many people:
"The Lord will stand beside the poor,
  To save them from those who condemn them to die."

PSALM 110

An oracle of the Lord to my Lord:
  "Sit at my right hand—I set up a throne,
    Your enemies are your footstool."
God sends forth your powerful scepter;
  The Lord will march from Zion.
God is with you in the midst of your foes;
  They are trophies for the day of your triumph.
In holy splendor, born of the Dawn,
  The dew of youth is yours.
The Lord swears, and does not revoke it:
  "You are a priest forever,
    The same as Melchizedek."
At your right hand, the Lord strikes;
  Today God is angry, my king!
God judges the nations, filling the valleys,
  Smashing high mountains, across the wide world.
The king drinks from God's mighty river;
  Therefore he lifts his head high.

PSALM 111

I will thank the Lord with all my heart,
  In the gathered assembly of the righteous;
Mighty are the deeds of the Lord,
  Studied by all who delight in them.

Majestic and splendid is God's work;
  God's justice will stand forever,
A monument to God's wonderful deeds;
  The Lord is compassion and grace.

Those who worship God will have food,
  In accord with the promise made long ago
When wonderful things were announced to God's people,
  That gave them the heritage of nations.
Faithful and just are the works of God's hands;
  Trustworthy are all God's decrees,
Standing forever and ever,
  Done with integrity and truth.

God has sent us redemption,
  And decreed an eternal covenant.
    Holy and awesome is God's name!
To worship the Lord is the highest wisdom;
  Those who do so know all that is good—
    God's praises will last forever.

PSALM 112

Happy are those who worship the Lord,
  And take great delight in God's commands.
Their children shall be the world's rulers,
  And be blessed in an age of justice.

Their homes will have wealth and plenty,
  And their justice last forever.
For the upright, a light shines in darkness;
  It is kind, and gracious, and just.

It is good to be kind and lend freely,
  To offer one's goods in the cause of justice.
Then you will never stumble;
  The fame of the just will last forever.

They do not fear evil rumors;
  Their hearts firmly trust in the Lord.
Their courage sustained, they have no fear;
  Soon they will triumph over their foes.

They give lavish gifts to the poor;
    Their justice will last forever.
        They lift up their heads in glory.
Transgressors will see and be angry—
    They gnash their teeth and pine away;
        Evil desires lead to ruin.

PSALM 113

Praise the Lord!
You, the Lord's servants, praise,
    Praise the name of the Lord.
Let the Lord's name be blessed
    From now on, and forever.
Wherever the sun shines, from dawn until dusk,
    Let the Lord's name be praised.
The Lord is high over all nations;
    Beyond the sky is God's glory.
Who is like the Lord our God,
    Enthroned so high above,
Yet stooping down in order to see
    What happens on earth and in heaven!
God lifts the oppressed from the dust,
    And raises the poor from the trash heap,
To set them among the nobles,
    The nobles of God's own people,
While women once barren have children,
    And rejoice in the homes God gives them.
Praise the Lord!

PSALM 114

When Israel came out from Egypt,
    Jacob's house, from a foreign land,
Judah became God's sanctuary,
    And Israel God's dominion.
The sea perceived this and fled;
    The Jordan reversed its flow.

The mountains skipped about like rams;
   The hills, like kids and lambs.
Sea, what happened to you, that you fled?
   Jordan, that you reversed your flow?
Mountains, that you skipped like rams,
   Like lambs and kids, you hills?
Writhe, O earth, in the sight of the Lord,
   In the sight of Jacob's God,
Who changes rock into pools of water,
   And flint into flowing springs.

PSALM 115

Not to us, Lord, but to your name
   Give honor because of your constant love.
Why should the nations say,
   "Where then is their God?"
Our God is in the sky;
   And whatever God wishes, is done.
All their idols are silver and gold,
   The works of human hands—
They have mouths, but they cannot speak,
   Eyes, but they cannot see,
Ears, but they cannot hear,
   Noses, but they cannot smell,
Hands, but they cannot feel,
   Feet, but they cannot walk;
      In their throats there is not a whisper.
Their makers will be just like them,
   Everyone who trusts in them.
But let Israel trust in the Lord,
   Who is their savior and shield;
Let the priests all trust in the Lord,
   Who is their savior and shield;
Let the people trust in the Lord,
   Who is their savior and shield;
      The Lord will remember to bless us.
God will bless the house of Israel;
   God will bless the priests like Aaron,

God will bless the people,
   Whether they are small or great.
God will again act on your behalf,
   And on behalf of your children.
You will be blessed by the Lord,
   Who makes the earth and the sky.
The highest heaven belongs to the Lord,
   Who gives the earth to Adam's descendants.
It is not the dead who praise the Lord—
   Not all those who go down to silence;
But we will bless the Lord,
   From now on, and forever.
Praise the Lord!

PSALM 116

I love you, Lord, because you hear
   The sound of my cry for help.
Your ear is attentive to me,
   In the days when I call to you.
Death's chains enclose me, death's torments have found me;
   I have been found by distress and trouble.
I call to the Lord by name,
   "Please, Lord, save my life!"
The Lord is just and gracious;
   Our God will act with compassion.
The Lord protects the common people;
   I am unimportant, but God will save me.
I will have inner peace again,
   For the Lord will act on my behalf.
For God will save me from death,
   My eyes from tears, my feet from stumbling.
And I will walk in the presence of God,
   Among those who live in this world.
Despite persecution, let me remain faithful,
   Submitting myself completely.
I see, with sudden fear,
   That all human beings are liars!

How can I repay you, Lord?
  You have acted on my behalf.
I will drink a toast to your saving power,
  And call out your name, O Lord.
To you, O Lord, I fulfill my vows
  In the presence of all your people.
How precious in your eyes, O Lord,
  Are those who die, faithful to you.
Please, Lord, unlock my chains;
  For I am your slave, as was my mother.
Offerings of thanks I will give to you,
  And call out your name, O Lord.
To you, O Lord, I fulfill my vows
  In the presence of all your people,
In the courts of your house, O Lord,
  In the midst of Jerusalem.

PSALM 117

Praise the Lord, all nations;
  All peoples, glorify God,
Whose grace, like a wave, surges over us,
  Whose faithfulness lasts for all time.
    Praise the Lord!

PSALM 118

Praise the Lord, who is good;
  God will be faithful forever.
Now declare this, Israel:
  "God will be faithful forever."
Declare this, you who are priests like Aaron:
  "God will be faithful forever."
Declare this, people who fear the Lord:
  "God will be faithful forever."

Hemmed in, I called to the Lord;
  In freedom, God answered me.
The Lord is with me; I will not fear.
  What can mortals do to me?

The Lord is with me and comes to help me;
  I look on my foes with disdain.
It is better to hide in the Lord
  Than to trust in mere human beings.
It is better to hide in the Lord
  Than to trust in earthly rulers.
All the nations enclosed me;
  In the name of the Lord I cut off their foreskins.
They had me completely surrounded;
  In the name of the Lord I cut off their foreskins.
They enclosed me like swarms of bees,
   Like a crackling fire of thornbush;
    In the name of the Lord I cut off their foreskins.
They nearly overwhelmed me,
  But the Lord delivered me.

The Lord is my strength and power,
  And became a savior to me.
Hear the triumphant shouting
  Resound in the tents of the victors!
The Lord's right hand was our power;
  The Lord's right hand was lifted high.
I did not die: I survived,
  To tell what the Lord has done.
In fact, the Lord dealt harshly with me,
  But did not give me up to death.
Open for me the gates of triumph;
  I will enter to praise the Lord.
This is the gate that leads to the Lord;
  Let the victors go through it!
I will praise you for answering me;
  You became a savior to me.
A stone that the builders rejected
  Has become the cornerstone;
This has come from the Lord—
  We couldn't imagine it!
This very day the Lord has acted;
  Let us shout and rejoice in God.

We beg you, Lord, to save us!
  We beg you, Lord, to make us prosper!

We bless you who come in the name of the Lord;
From the Lord's own temple, we bless you.
Truly the Lord's light shines upon us!
Form the lines for the festal procession
Up to the horns of the altar.

You are my God; I praise you.
My God, I raise you high.
Praise the Lord, who is good;
God will be faithful forever.

PSALM 119

A Happy are those whose conduct is perfect,
Who walk by the Lord's instruction.
Happy are those who obey God's counsels,
Seeking God with all their heart.
Truly, they do nothing wicked;
They walk in the ways of God.
You have commanded us
Strictly to follow your orders.
Just let my steps be firm,
That I may obey your decrees;
Then I will not be ashamed
When I contemplate your commands.
With clear heart and mind I will praise you,
As I study your just decisions.
I will obey your decrees;
Do not completely forsake me.

B How can a youth act clearly?
By keeping to what you say!
I have sought you with all my heart—
Keep me close to what you command.
I store your word in my mind,
Lest I should sin against you.
Blessed are you, O Lord;
Teach me your decrees.
With my own lips I recite
Every verdict your mouth has spoken.

I delight in the path you advise,
  More than in all kinds of wealth.
I meditate on your orders,
  And try to see all your ways.
I rejoice in what you decree;
  I will never forget your word.

G   Act on behalf of your servant;
      I will live, obeying your word.
    Open my eyes; let me see
      The wonders of your instruction.
    Do not hide your commands from me,
      A stranger in this land;
    I have worn myself out completely,
      Always desiring your judgment.
    May you curse and rebuke the arrogant,
      Who wander from your commands.
    Remove my shame and disgrace,
      For I have observed your warnings.
    There sit the rulers who speak against me,
      While I, your servant, attend to your tasks.
    Your admonitions are truly my joy,
      And they alone will direct me.

D   I feel trapped, and worthless, and dry;
      Give me life, as you have promised.
    When I say how I want to proceed,
      Let me know what you have determined.
    Explain the way you direct me;
      I will ponder your marvelous deeds.
    My body stoops in sorrow;
      Lift me up as you have promised.
    Keep me far from ways that mislead;
      Graciously give me your teaching.
    I have chosen the honest way,
      Letting your judgments rule me.
    I cling to your admonitions, Lord;
      Do not humiliate me.
    Let me run the course you command;
      It is you who can make me bold.

E   Instruct me, Lord, in the way you decree,
     And I will completely obey.
   Show me your teaching, and I will comply,
     And keep it with all my heart.
   Make me go by the path you command;
     In so doing is my delight.
   Bend my will to your direction,
     And not to selfish advantage.
   Do not let me exist for no purpose;
     Let me live in accord with your ways.
   Fulfill your word to your servant,
     So that I may worship you.
   I fear that disgrace is coming to me;
     In your good judgment, prevent it.
   I only desire to follow your orders;
     Let me live by your just purpose.

W   Let your mercies come to me, Lord,
     The salvation that you have promised.
   Then I will answer any who taunt me,
     For I can trust your word.
   Don't take the truth from my mouth,
     For I await your judgment.
   I will keep to your instruction,
     Constantly and forever.
   Let me walk in spacious places,
     For I seek direction from you;
   And let me speak of your warnings,
     Shamelessly, before kings.
   Let your commands be my joy,
     For they are what I love;
   And so I salute your commands,
     And attend to your decrees.

Z   Remember your word to your servant,
     The reason I wait for you.
   It is my comfort in sorrow
     That what you say gives me life.
   The terrible scorn of the proud
     Will not turn me away from your teaching.
   I remember your ancient judgments;

By them, Lord, I am consoled.
Rage at transgressors grips me;
   They have abandoned your teaching.
Your decrees are music to me,
   In the house where I live as a stranger.
I remember your name in the night, Lord,
   And your teaching in the dark hours.
This is what has become of me
   Because I obeyed your orders.

H   You are my sustenance, Lord;
   I have promised to do what you say.
I most humbly seek your favor;
   Be gracious, as you have promised.
I consider all my ways,
   Redirecting my steps as you urge me.
I hurry, I do not delay,
   To obey your commandments.
Though the snares of the guilty surround me,
   I do not forget your instruction.
I rise at midnight to praise you
   For your unimpeachable judgments.
All who obey your orders
   And fear you are my companions.
O Lord, your grace fills the world;
   Teach me your decrees.

I   You have been good to your servant,
   Just as you promised, O Lord.
Teach me insight and knowledge;
   I completely trust your commandments.
I could only do wrong until I surrendered,
   But now I obey your word.
How kind and gracious you are!
   Teach me your decrees.
Insolent people smear me with lies,
   But I follow your orders with all my heart.
Their hearts, like lard, have no feeling;
   But I make your instruction my joy.
It was good that you subdued me,
   So that I might learn your decrees.

The instruction you speak is more precious to me
    Than heaps of silver and gold.

J   Your hands have made and upheld me;
    Give me insight, to learn your commands.
Those who fear you will see me and celebrate,
    For I have awaited your word.
I know, O Lord, that your judgments are just,
    And you were right to subdue me;
But now let your love console me,
    As you have promised your servant.
And let your compassion come to me;
    I will live by my joy in your teaching.
Shame those insolent frauds who deceived me,
    And let me attend to your decrees.
Let those who fear you return to me,
    And those who know that you guide them.
Let me set my mind wholly on your demands,
    So that shame may not come to me.

K   I commit myself to your saving power,
    And I will await your word.
My eyes are straining to see your purpose,
    As I ask, "When will you comfort me?"
Though I wander as if in a fog,
    I do not forget your decrees.
How long must your servant await your judgment?
    When will you act against those who hound me?
They boldly dig pits to trap me,
    Completely against your teaching.
All your commands are reliable;
    But these liars pursue me—help me!
They soon will force me out of this world,
    Yet I do not forsake your decrees.
Let me live, in accord with your grace;
    And let me obey your summons.

L   You are eternal, O Lord,
    And your word governs the skies.
You are trustworthy, age after age;
    You constructed the world to stand firm.

All these things stand today by your judgment,
  For all of them are your servants.
If your teaching had not been my joy,
  Then I would have perished in misery.
Never will I ignore your orders,
  For by them you bring me to life.
Save me, for I am yours;
  For I have sought your directions.
The wicked wait for a chance to destroy me,
  But I am attentive to your admonitions.
I have seen the limits of all finite things,
  But your commandment is so unbounded!

M How I love your instruction!
     I devote myself to it all day.
   Your command makes me wiser than all my foes;
     And indeed it is mine forever!
   I have more understanding than all my teachers,
     For I contemplate your covenant.
   I have keener insight than the elders,
     For I have obeyed your orders.
   I restrain my feet from all evil paths,
     So that I may obey your word.
   I do not turn aside from your judgments,
     For it is you who instruct me.
   How smooth to my palate is all that you say;
     To my mouth it is sweeter than honey.
   From your directions I train my mind,
     And so I hate every false way.

N Your word is a lamp for my journey,
     A light along my path;
   And I will fulfill my vow
     To obey your righteous judgments.
   How greatly mortified I am!
     Let me live, Lord, as you have promised.
   When I speak my own mind, Lord, be patient;
     Teach me your judgments.
   I am constantly risking my life,
     But I never forget your instruction.
   Though the wicked set snares for me,

I will not stray from your orders.
Because my heart's joy is your covenant,
   I accept it as my eternal heritage.
I stretch my mind to do as you prescribe,
   To the end of time.

S   I hate those who waver and hesitate,
   But how I love your instruction!
You are my refuge and shield;
   I await your word.
Get away from me, you who harm me,
   And let me obey my God's commands!
God, sustain my life, as you promised;
   Do not make me ashamed of my hope.
Uphold me, and I will be saved;
   I will always respond to your summons.
You care nothing for all who ignore your decrees,
   Lost in their vain speculations.
You remove the earth's exploiters, like dross;
   That is why I love your admonitions—
Though my every hair bristles in fear,
   And I am in awe of your judgments.

O   I have done what is just and right;
   Do not leave me to my oppressors!
Commit yourself to your servant's welfare;
   Do not let the proud oppress me.
My eyes are straining to see your salvation,
   To see the justice you promise.
Deal with me in your grace,
   And teach me your decrees.
I am your slave—give me insight,
   And make me aware of your covenant.
It is time to act, O Lord!
   They are subverting your teaching!
But as I have said, I love your commands
   More than jewels and gold.
Precisely as you direct, I proceed,
   And so I hate every false way.

P   Your admonitions are wonderful;
   So I keep them with all my heart.

What light is disclosed by your word,
  Giving insight to those who were foolish!
As if I were panting, openmouthed,
  I yearn for your commandments.
Turn to me, and give me your grace,
  Your assurance for those who love you.
Make my steps firm in your word;
  Let sin have no power against me.
Redeem me from human oppressors,
  And I will obey your orders.
Let your face shine on your servant,
  And teach me your decrees.
Streams flow down from my eyes
  For those who dishonor your teaching.

Z Truly, O Lord, you are righteous,
    Correct in all your judgments.
  You rightly demand our obedience,
    And our utmost fidelity.
  You silence my jealous complaining
    That those who oppress me dishonor your teaching.
  Your word is refined in a mighty fire,
    And I, your servant, adore it!
  Unimportant and scorned as I am,
    I never forget your decrees.
  How eternally just is your judgment!
    How dependable your instruction!
  Harsh distress has come to me;
    Your commandments remain my delight.
  Forever just are your admonitions;
    Give me insight, and let me live.

Q I cry out with all my heart,
    "Answer me, Lord; I will follow your orders!"
  I cry out to you, "Deliver me;
    I will honor your admonitions!"
  I start pleading for help before it is light;
    I wait for your word.
  In the dark before dawn I open my eyes,
    To ponder all that you say.

In your grace, O Lord, hear my voice;
   In your justice, make me alive.
As my cunning pursuers approach me,
   They get farther away from your teaching.
But you, O Lord, be near me!
   Let all your commands be effective!
Long have I heeded the admonitions
   That you have established forever.

R See my affliction, and save me;
   For I never forget your teaching.
Plead my case, and redeem me;
   Let me live, as you have promised.
Salvation is far away from the wicked,
   Who care nothing about your decrees.
You are so compassionate, Lord;
   In your justice, make me alive.
Those who hound and oppress me are many;
   But I don't neglect your warnings.
I see deceivers, and loathe them
   For disobeying your word.
See how I love your directions;
   Lord, let me live by your grace.
First and foremost, your word is true,
   And your judgment is always right.

S For no reason, princes persecute me.
   My heart trembles whenever you speak.
From your word I receive more joy
   Than from carrying off great plunder.
I hate and abhor deception,
   But your instruction I love.
Seven times daily I praise you,
   Because of your righteous judgments.
Serene are those who love your teaching;
   Nothing unsettles them.
My hope, Lord, is your salvation;
   I will do what you command.
My whole self loves and obeys
   Your covenant stipulations.
I obey your covenant orders;
   All my motives are clear to you.

T   Let my cry come before you, O Lord;
    Give me insight, as you have promised.
Let my plea come into your presence;
    Rescue me in accord with your word.
Praise will bubble out of my mouth
    Whenever you teach me your will.
When you speak, my tongue will respond,
    For all your commands are righteous.
May your own hand support me;
    I have chosen to follow your orders.
I long for your saving power;
    O Lord, I rejoice in your teaching.
I myself will live to praise you,
    And your judgments will come to my aid.
Seek your servant, a sheep lost and dying,
    Who never forgot your commandments.

PSALM 120

To you, Lord, when I was oppressed,
    I called and you answered me:
"O Lord, please save my life
    From liar's lips, from tricksters' tongues."
What will come to you, over and over,
    You with the trickster's tongue—
Sharp arrows from heroes' bows,
    And searing coals of fire!

I feel like a stranger in savage lands,
    Living among barbarians.
Too long have I lived among those who hate peace;
    When I speak of peace, they are all for war.

PSALM 121

I look at the hills, and wonder
    From where will my help come?
My help comes from the Lord,
    The maker of earth and sky.

May God not let you stumble;
   May God your protector not sleep!
Truly God never rests or sleeps,
   Protecting Israel.
The Lord is your protector,
   The shade at your right hand.
The sun will not strike you by day,
   Nor the moon at night.
The Lord protects you from every evil;
   God protects your life.
The Lord will protect you, coming and going,
   Now, and forevermore.

PSALM 122

I was glad when they said to me,
   "Come with us to the house of the Lord!"
And now we are standing here,
   Within your gates, Jerusalem.
The city Jerusalem, strongly built—
   To this place the tribes come up,
The Lord's tribes, the assembly of Israel,
   To praise the name of the Lord.
For here stood the thrones of judgment,
   The thrones of David's successors.

Pray for the peace of Jerusalem!
   "Give rest to those who love you;
Let peace be within your walls,
   Quiet within your towers.
For the sake of my family and friends,
   Let me speak for your well-being;
For the sake of the house of the Lord our God,
   Let me seek what is best for you."

PSALM 123

I lift up my eyes to you,
   God, enthroned in the sky.

As slaves who acknowledge their master's power,
　As a maid who looks to her mistress,
So we will look to you, Lord,
　Until you show us your grace.
Be gracious to us, Lord, be gracious!
　We have had too much of contempt;
Too long have we had to live
　With the scorn of the smug, the contempt of the proud.

PSALM 124

"Had it not been the Lord who was for us,"
　Recite it now, Israel—
Had it not been the Lord who was for us,
　When the whole world rose against us,
They would have swallowed us alive,
　When their anger ignited against us;
The flood would have washed us away,
　The torrent would have swept over us—
It would have swept our lives away,
　That raging, arrogant flood!

But blessed be the Lord,
　Who did not let us be prey for their teeth!
The trap is broken; our lives are saved,
　Like birds that escape from the fowler's snare.
Our help is in the name of the Lord,
　The maker of earth and sky.

PSALM 125

Those who trust in the Lord are like Mount Zion,
　Which never totters, standing forever.
The mountains surround Jerusalem,
　As you, Lord, surround your people,
　　From now on and forever.

God will not let the oppressor's rod
　Rule over the fate of the righteous,

Lest the righteous begin to use
   Their strength for unjust ends.
Do good, Lord, to those who are good,
   Whose hearts are intent on justice.
But banish distorted powers,
   Along with those who wield them.
     And let Israel be at peace.

PSALM 126

When the Lord shall again set Zion free—
   Let us be as dreamers—
Then laughter will fill our mouths,
   And our tongues will shout for joy.
They will say among the nations,
   "The Lord has done great things for them!"
May the Lord do great things for us,
   And then may we rejoice!

Lord, bring back our exiles,
   Like streams to water the desert.
Those who sow with tears—
   May they gather the harvest with singing.
True, they may go out weeping,
   Bearing a pouch of seed;
But let them return with laughter,
   Bearing their sheaves of grain!

PSALM 127

If the Lord does not build the house,
   In vain do the builders labor.
If the Lord does not guard the city,
   In vain is the sentry's vigil.
In vain do you rise before dawn,
   And stay up into the night;
By diligent work you eat bread
   Which God's loved ones receive while sleeping!

Truly, sons are God's gift;
   God's reward is the fruit of the womb.
The sons that are born to young men
   Are the arrows in heroes' hands;
Happy the man who has filled
   His quiver full of them!
Unabashed, they defeat in the village assembly
   The adversaries who sue them.

PSALM 128

Happy the man who fears the Lord,
   Who walks in God's ways;
You will eat what your labor produces,
   And be happy and prosperous.
Your wife will be like a fruitful vine,
   At the corner of your home;
Your children, like olive shoots,
   Will grow around your table.
This blessing comes to the man who fears God;
   The Lord will bless you from Zion.
May you see Jerusalem prosper,
   All the days of your life;
May you see your children's children,
   And may Israel be at peace.

PSALM 129

"They have greatly oppressed me since I was young,"
   Recite it now, Israel—
They have greatly oppressed me since I was young,
   Yet they have not overcome me.
They scored my back as if with plows;
   They made the furrows deep and long.
But the Lord, in justice, cut to pieces
   The ropes with which they cruelly bound me.
And all who hated Zion drew back,
   In utter humiliation.

They are like grass on the rooftops—
  A dry east wind, and it withers;
No reapers get even a handful,
  Much less gather their sheaves!
No passerby speaks the Lord's blessing to them!
  No one says, "Bless you, in the Lord's name."

PSALM 130

From the depths I cry to you;
  Lord, listen to my voice.
Let your ear be open
  To the sound of my plea for pardon.

Lord, if you keep account of wrongs,
  Who will be able to stand?
But you are prepared to forgive us,
  That we may worship you.

My inmost self longs for the Lord;
  I wait for the word of God.
I tell myself, "Wait for the Lord
  As a sentry watches for morning."
As a sentry watches for morning,
  Israel, wait for the Lord.

Surely the Lord will be faithful,
  And redeem us again and again.
God will redeem Israel
  From all our guilty deeds.

PSALM 131

Lord, I do not intend to be haughty;
  I do not want to aim too high.
I am not concerned with impressive things,
  Or with problems unsuited to me.
Have I not calmed and stilled my inner self?
  I rest on God, as an infant rests on its mother.

Israel, wait for the Lord,
  From now on, and forever.

PSALM 132

Remember David, O Lord,
  And all his humility;
The vow he made to the Lord,
  His oath to the Bull of Jacob.
"I will never go inside my house,
  Never lie down on my bed,
Never give sleep to my eyes,
  Nor allow my eyelids to close,
Until I find a place for the Lord,
  A dwelling for Jacob's Bull."
We heard of this in Bethlehem;
  We found it out in Field Forest.
Let us go to the Lord's own dwelling;
  Let us bow at the footstool of God.
Arise, O Lord, from your resting place—
  You and the Ark of your power.
Let justice clothe your priests;
  Let the faithful shout for joy.
For the sake of your servant David,
  Do not reject your Messiah.
The Lord, having sworn to David,
  Will certainly never turn back!
"I establish a throne for you,
  And for those who are born of your seed.
If your sons will keep my covenant,
  The agreement I will teach them,
Then your sons, forever and ever,
  Will sit upon your throne."
For the Lord has chosen Zion;
  God desires to live there.
"Here is my home forever and ever;
  Here I will live, as I desire.
I will greatly bless Jerusalem's pilgrims,
  And provide Zion's poor with food.

I will clothe her priests in salvation;
   The faithful people will laugh and shout.
Here will I cultivate David's power,
   And prepare my Messiah's lamp.
I will clothe his foes in shame,
   But for David himself—a splendid crown!"

PSALM 133

Ah, how good and lovely it is
   For brothers and sisters to live in community!
Like fragrant oil upon one's head,
   Flowing down one's beard,
The beard of Aaron, flowing down
   The collar of his robes;
Like the dew of Mount Hermon, coming down
   Upon the hills of Zion—
There the Lord confers the blessing,
   Life that lasts forever.

PSALM 134

Come bless the Lord,
   All you, the Lord's servants,
Who are in the Lord's house
   Both day and night.
Raise your hands toward the temple,
   And bless the Lord;
The Lord, who makes earth and sky,
   Will bless you from Mount Zion.

PSALM 135

Praise the Lord!
Praise the Lord's name;
   Praise, you the Lord's servants,
Who stand in the house of the Lord,
   In the courts of the house of our God.

Praise the Lord, who is good;
  Sing God's beautiful name.
For it is Jacob that God has chosen;
  Israel is God's precious possession.
I know that the Lord is great;
  Our God is greater than all other gods.
On earth, or in the skies,
  In all the depths of the sea,
    Whatever pleases the Lord is done—
God brings the mist from the world's far corners;
  God makes the lightning precede the rain,
    And brings the wind out of the storehouse.
It is God who slew Egypt's eldest sons,
  Among the cattle as well as the people;
Who sent miraculous omens—
  Into your midst, O Egypt!—
    Against Pharaoh and all his slaves.
It is God who slew great nations,
  And slaughtered mighty kings—
Sihon, the Amorite king,
  Og, the king of Bashan,
    And all the rulers of Canaan.
It is God who bequeathed their land,
  Bequeathed it to Israel, God's own people.
The Lord is your name forever;
  We address you as Lord age after age.
For you will plead your people's cause;
  You will avenge your servants.
The gentiles have idols of silver and gold,
  Made by human hands.
They have mouths, but are speechless,
  And eyes, but are blind.
They have ears, yet hear nothing;
  Their mouths are devoid of the breath of life.
Their makers will be just like them,
  And so will all their believers!
O house of Israel, bless the Lord!
  You priests like Aaron, bless the Lord.
You descendants of Levi, bless the Lord.
  You who worship the Lord, bless the Lord.

Blessed be the Lord, who comes from Zion,
  The God who lives in Jerusalem.
Praise the Lord!

PSALM 136

Praise to the Lord, who is good,
  Whose grace is everlasting.
Praise to the God of gods,
  Whose grace is everlasting.
Praise to the Lord of lords,
  Whose grace is everlasting.
Who alone does mighty deeds,
  Whose grace is everlasting.
Who made the skies in wisdom,
  Whose grace is everlasting.
Who stretched the earth over the seas,
  Whose grace is everlasting.
Who made the great sources of light—
  Whose grace is everlasting.
The sun that governs the day,
  Whose grace is everlasting.
The moon and stars that rule the night,
  Whose grace is everlasting.
Who struck down Egypt's eldest sons,
  Whose grace is everlasting.
And brought Israel out from among them,
  Whose grace is everlasting.
With strong hand and outstretched arm,
  Whose grace is everlasting.
Who split the Red Sea apart,
  Whose grace is everlasting.
That God's people might walk on dry ground,
  Whose grace is everlasting.
Who brought Israel through the midst of the water,
  Whose grace is everlasting.
And tossed Pharaoh's army into the sea,
  Whose grace is everlasting.
Who struck down kings in their power,
  Whose grace is everlasting.

And slaughtered kings in their might—
  Whose grace is everlasting.
Sihon, the Amorite king,
  Whose grace is everlasting.
And Og, the king of Bashan,
  Whose grace is everlasting.
Who made a bequest of their land,
  Whose grace is everlasting.
A bequest to Israel, God's own servant,
  Whose grace is everlasting.
Who in our subjection remembered us,
  Whose grace is everlasting.
And rescued us from our oppressors,
  Whose grace is everlasting.
Who still feeds every creature,
  Whose grace is everlasting.
Praise to the God of the skies,
  Whose grace is everlasting.

PSALM 137

There by Babylon's rivers,
  We sat weeping aloud,
    And we remembered Zion;
On the poplars there,
  We hung up our lyres.
But what did they ask from us?
  Our captors asked us to sing!
Our tormentors cried, "Entertain us!
  Sing to us from the songs of Zion!"

How can we sing the Lord's song,
  Here on foreign soil?
Jerusalem, should I forget you,
  Let my right hand shrivel;
Let my tongue stick to my palate,
  Should I fail to remember you.
Oh, let me go up to Jerusalem,
  Wearing once more a festal crown!

Lord, recall against Edom's people
  The day Jerusalem fell.

"Strip it, lay it bare," they said,
  "Right to its foundation."
As for you, Babylon, ripe for destruction,
  Happy the one who avenges
    The deed you did to us—
Happy the one who seizes your children
  To smash them against a cliff.

PSALM 138

I will praise you with all my heart;
  I will sing to you, sovereign God.
I will bow down to your holy temple,
  And praise you for what you are.
As for your steadfast fidelity,
  You surpass your own reputation.
On the day I called, you answered me;
  You multiplied strength in my weak self.
All the world's rulers will praise you, Lord,
  For they have heard the words of your mouth;
And they will sing of the ways of the Lord,
  For the glory of God is great.
Though high above, God regards the humble;
  Though exalted, the Lord sees from far away.
If I walk right into terrible dangers,
  You make me live, in spite of my foes.
You reach out, and your right hand saves me;
  The Lord takes vengeance on my behalf.
Lord, your fidelity lasts forever;
  Do not abandon the work of your hands!

PSALM 139

Lord, you have searched and known me;
  You know my deeds and my thoughts,
    Discerning my purpose far in advance.
You mark each digression and pause,
  Familiar with all my habits.

There is not a word on my tongue
  Before you know it completely.
Front and back you enclose me,
  And place your hand upon me.
How can I comprehend such wonders,
  So far beyond my grasp!

Where could I go, away from your Spirit?
  Where could I flee from your presence?
If I climbed the skies, you'd be there;
  If I lay down in Hades, I'd meet you.
If I took the wings of the dawn,
  To go live beyond the sea,
There, too, your hand would lead me,
  Your right hand hold me fast.
I might say, "Darkness has snatched me away;
  Night encloses me all around!"
But darkness is not too dark for you—
  You cause the night to shine like day.

For you created my inmost parts;
  You wove me within my mother's womb.
I praise you, God—how awesome you are—
  You make me so unique, as are all your creatures!
You have known my true self forever;
  Nothing about me is hidden from you.
It is you who made me in secret;
  In the depths of the earth you knit me together.
You foresaw each stage of my life;
  They were all written down in your scroll.
You kept track of all my days,
  Before I had even appeared.
O God, how highly you thought of me;
  How great is the sum of your plans!
I could no more count them than grains of sand;
  Just let me awake, and still be with you.

If only you would slay the wicked!
  Make those murderers leave me alone!
They think they are more crafty than you,
  And use your inspirations for idle ends.

Lord, I hate those who hate you—
  I despise their rebellion against you!
My hatred for them is complete;
  I consider them personal foes.
Explore me, God, and know my heart;
  Test me and know my disquieting thoughts.
Look for destructive ways in me,
  And lead me in ways that endure.

PSALM 140

Save me, O Lord, from cruel people,
  Guard me from their violence.
They plan cruel deeds in their hearts;
  Their warlike attacks come all day long.
They sharpen their tongues like serpents;
  Behind their lips is the viper's poison.
Protect me, Lord, from their evil power;
  Guard me from their violence.
    They plan to trip up my feet.
They boldly conceal a trap for me,
  And stretch out the cords of their net.
    Along the road they set snares for me.

I say, "Lord, you are my God;
  Hear the sound of my cry for help."
Lord God, my saving strength,
  Protect my head on the day of battle.
Do not allow them their evil desires;
  Nor grant them the outcome they plan.
All around me are the proud,
  Who hide behind heaps of words.
Drop coals of fire upon them;
  Plunge them into the abyss forever!
Don't let clever speech keep them safe in this world;
  Let evil harass and pursue these cruel people!
I know that you will act, O Lord;
  Your verdict will be for the wretched and poor.
Then the victors will praise your name,
  And the guiltless will live in your presence.

PSALM 141

I call you, Lord; hurry to me!
  Hear my voice when I call to you.
Let my prayer be incense before you,
  My lifted hands an evening sacrifice.

Set a sentry, O Lord, at my mouth,
  A guard at the door of my lips.
Don't let me dwell on evil thoughts,
    Or carry them out in guilty deeds,
      With people who do what is wrong.
I don't want to share their sumptuous feasts.
    Let them beat me for being righteous,
      Or criticize me for my faith,
But don't let their ointment shine on my head;
  Let my prayers forever oppose their schemes.
Let their leaders be smashed on a rock,
  And let them hear these fair words of mine!

As though I were cut down, hacked to pieces,
  My bones are strewn at Sheol's door.
Yet I look to you, Lord God;
  I await you; don't leave me to die!
Save me from all their traps,
  From the snares of those who do wrong.
Let the wicked fall into their own nets;
  Then I will be able to slip away.

PSALM 142

I cry aloud to the Lord;
  To the Lord I plead aloud for grace.
I pour my concern out before you;
  I declare my distress in your presence.
My spirit is fainting within me—
  But you know the path I have taken.
Along the road I travel,
  They have set traps for me!

Please be willing to notice me;
  No one looks out for me.
I have no place to hide,
  And no one cares if I live or die.
I cry out to you, O Lord;
  "You are my refuge," I say;
    "You are all I have in this world."
Respond to my moaning cry—
  How very small I am!
Save me from my pursuers,
  For they are stronger than I.
Bring me out of my prison,
  And let me praise your name.
Let the righteous be my companions,
  When you have brought me through.

PSALM 143

Listen to my prayer, O Lord;
  Hear me plead for your grace.
    Surely you will answer me!
I am your slave; do not accuse me!
  For no living person is blameless before you.
My enemy seeks to kill me;
  My life is crushed to the ground.
    Bring me back from the dark of eternal death.
My spirit grows more and more feeble;
  My heart is numb within me.
I remember days long past—
  I reflect on all your deeds,
    Considering what your hands have done.
Weary as a deserted land,
  I reach out my hand to you.
Answer me quickly, O Lord;
  My spirit is wasting away.
Do not hide your face from me;
  I will be like those who descend to the grave.
Declare your grace to me in the morning;
  I put my trust in you.

Tell me the way I should go,
   For my life depends on you.
Save me, O Lord, from my foes;
   Let me hide myself in you.
Teach me to do what pleases you,
   For you are my God.
Let your good spirit guide me
   To a level and righteous country.
Because you are the Lord, give me life;
   In your justice, bring me out from oppression.
Silence my foes in your mercy,
   Exterminate those who oppress me.
     For I am your slave.

PSALM 144

Blessed be the Lord, my mountain,
   Who teaches me how to do battle,
     And readies my hands for war.
My friend and my mountain fortress,
   My tower and place of refuge,
In God, my shield, I have confidence;
   It is God who makes my people obey me.
O Lord, we are human, yet you befriend us;
   Mere mortals, yet you consider us.
People are like a passing sigh,
   Their days like a shadow that slips away.
Leave your skies, O Lord, and come down;
   Touch the mountains, and let them smolder!
Let lightning flash, to scatter my foes;
   Fire your bow; let them flee in confusion.
Send your power down from on high;
   Rescue me from mighty torrents,
     And save me from foreign peoples.
In their mouths are lying words;
   Their right hands deal out treachery.
O God, I will sing a new song to you,
   Playing a ten-stringed harp for you.
It is you who make kings victorious;
   You rescued David, your servant.

Rescue me from the deadly sword;
  Save me from the foreigners' power.

Let our sons be thriving saplings,
  Growing tall while they are young.
Make our daughters fluted pillars,
  Standing as though in a palace.
Let our storehouses be filled,
  With treasure of every kind.
Let our flocks be multiplied,
  Ten thousandfold in all our fields,
    With all our herds well-fed.
Keep us safe from siege and exile;
  Let no mourning wails be heard in our streets.
Happy the people for whom it is so!
  Happy the people whose God is the Lord!

PSALM 145

I will lift you high, my sovereign God,
  And bless your name, forever and always.
Every day I will bless you,
  And praise your name, forever and always.
The Lord is great, and much to be praised;
  God's greatness is never completely known.
Age after age will praise your works,
  And tell about your powers.
They will speak of your high and majestic splendor,
  And I will contemplate your wonders.
They will talk of your terrifying strength,
  And I will recount your greatest deeds.
They will tell stirring tales of your great goodness,
  And sing about your righteousness.
Compassion and grace—that is the Lord;
  Slow to be angry, determined to love us.
Lord, you are good to everyone,
  And compassionate to all your creatures.
All your creatures praise you, Lord;
  All your faithful people bless you.

They talk of your glorious sovereignty,
    And speak of your power,
Letting all humanity know of your power,
    Your high and glorious sovereignty.
Your royal rule lasts through all ages;
    Your dominion extends to all generations.
Every word you speak is true,
    And you are gracious to all your creatures.
The Lord supports everyone who is falling,
    And raises up everyone who is bent down.
Everyone looks to you in hope,
    And at the right time you provide their food.
You open up your hand,
    And fulfill the desire of each living thing.
Lord, you are righteous in all your ways,
    And faithful to all your creatures.
The Lord is near everyone who calls,
    Everyone who calls out in faith.
You do what your worshippers need from you;
    You hear their cry for help, and save them.
Lord, you watch over all who love you,
    And exterminate all the guilty.
My mouth will speak the Lord's praise;
    Let everyone bless God's holy name.

PSALM 146

Praise the Lord!
    My inmost self, praise the Lord,
Praise the Lord as long as I live;
    I will constantly sing to my God.
Do not depend on the noblest people,
    For no human power can save you.
Their breath departs; they return to the ground;
    On that very day their plans will perish.
Happy are those whose helper is Jacob's God,
    Whose hope is in God the Lord—
The maker of earth and sky and sea,
    And all the things that are in them;

Who always does what is right,
  Who brings justice to all the oppressed.
The Lord, who gives food to the famished,
  The Lord, who sets the prisoner free,
The Lord, who gives sight to the blind,
  The Lord, who lifts up the humbled,
The Lord, who loves those who act justly,
  The Lord, who protects the refugees,
Who comes to the aid of the orphan and widow,
  But subverts the plans of evil people.
The Lord will always rule,
  Your God, O Zion, forevermore.

PSALM 147

Praise the Lord!
How good it is to sing to our God!
  How suitable is beautiful praise!
Jerusalem's builder is the Lord,
  Who gathers Israel's scattered people,
Who heals the brokenhearted,
  And binds up their painful wounds;
Who counts the myriad stars,
  And calls them all by name.
Our Lord is great, and supremely strong,
  And infinite in wisdom.
The Lord helps the poor to arise,
  But drives the oppressors down to the ground.
Let us return thanks to the Lord,
  And sing with a harp to our God,
Who covers the sky with clouds,
  Who prepares the rain for the earth,
Who makes the mountains grow grass
  And green plants, to meet human needs;
Who gives to the cattle their feed,
  To young crows, the food they demand.
God takes no delight in a horse's strength,
  And is not pleased with muscular men;
It is those who wait in solemn fear,
  Trusting in grace, who please the Lord.

Jerusalem, glorify the Lord;
  Zion, praise your God,
Who strengthens the bars of your gates,
  And blesses the children within you;
Who makes your country prosperous,
  And satisfies you with plump grain;
Whose command directs the world,
  Whose word runs so swiftly;
Who sends the snow, heaped up like wool,
  Who scatters the frost like dust,
Who hurls down icy bits of hail—
  Can anyone stand before God's bitter cold?
But God speaks again, and all of it melts;
  God turns the wind, and the waters flow.
It is this God who spoke to Jacob,
  Who commanded and judged Israel,
But God did so for no other nation—
  They do not know God's decrees.
Praise the Lord!

PSALM 148

Praise the Lord! Hallelujah!
Praise God from the sky,
  Praise God from the heights;
Praise God, all you angels,
  Praise God, heaven's armies.
Praise God, sun and moon,
  Praise God, all bright stars;
Praise God, skies above,
  And waters above the skies.
They praise their true Lord,
  Who ordered their making,
Who placed them for ever,
  In the courses they follow.

Praise the Lord from the earth,
  Ocean deeps and dragons,
Fire and hail, snow and smoke,
  Gale wind doing God's word;

All mountains and hills,
　All fruit trees and cedars,
All beasts, wild or tame,
　Creeping things and soaring birds;
All earth's kings and peoples,
　All earth's princes and rulers,
Young women and men,
　And the old with the young.
Praise the name of the Lord;
　God alone is worthy of honor.
God's might is above earth and sky;
　God's people rise up in power.
Israel's children are close to God,
　God the glory of all faithful people!
Praise the Lord! Hallelujah!

PSALM 149

Praise the Lord!
Sing a new song to the Lord;
　Sing praise in the faithful assembly.
Delight, Israel, in what God has done;
　Let Zion's children shout to their king.
Let them praise their true Lord with a dance,
　And sing to God with drum and harp.
For they are the people loved by the Lord,
　Who lifts up the poor in triumph.
Let people of faith rejoice in God's glory;
　And shout for joy, wherever they live.
God's praise in their mouths,
　Two-edged swords in their hands,
Doing vengeance among the nations,
　And judgment among the peoples;
Binding their kings with chains,
　Their nobles with fetters of iron,
Judging them by the letter of the law;
　Such is the triumph of God's faithful people.
Praise the Lord!

PSALM 150

Praise God in the earthly temple;
  Praise God in heaven's great dome.
Praise God the mighty hero;
  Praise God, supremely great.
Praise God with blasting trumpets;
  Praise God with harps and lyres.
Praise God with drums and dancing;
  Praise God with strings and flutes.
Praise God with sounding cymbals;
  Praise God with clamorous joy.
Let all who breathe, praise the Lord.
  Praise the Lord, Hallelujah!

Index of the Psalms

About the Author

The primary aim of Gary Chamberlain's fifteen years in the parish ministry has been to build bridges between modern biblical scholarship and local parish practice. Having served several congregations on the coast of Maine, he is now teaching biblical studies at the University of Dubuque Theological Seminary in Dubuque, Iowa.

Because of his interest in the psalms, Gary Chamberlain has worked with the original biblical texts in Hebrew and Greek, not only in worship preparation, but also in devotional reading. For a time, he followed the hours for prayer in the Rule of St. Benedict, using the psalms in Hebrew. As a result, he describes himself as "the only Methodist Benedictine rabbi in history."

Gary Chamberlain has an ongoing interest in poetry, both ancient and modern, and finds the work with the psalms has given his poetic and musical interests a practical application he had not anticipated. The book *Psalms for Singing*, also published by The Upper Room, presents twenty-six of Chamberlain's psalm translations with musical settings for congregation and choir.

Gary Chamberlain received the B.A. degree from Bates Colleges, Lewiston, Maine; the M.Div. degree from Bangor Theological Seminary; and the Ph.D. from Boston University.